I Didn't K...
ALMANAC

SOUTHERN EDITION
2007

COOL SPRINGS PRESS
A Division of Thomas Nelson Publishers
Since 1798

www.thomasnelson.com

Nashville, Tennessee

I DIDN'T KNOW THAT ALMANAC SOUTHERN EDITION 2007

Published by Cool Springs Press, a division of Thomas Nelson, Inc., P.O. Box 141000, Nashville, Tennessee, 37214.

First Printing 2006
Printed in the United States of America

Cover Design: Bruce Gore, Gore Studios
Writer: Jamie Chavez for WordWorks; additional writing by Dayle Fergusson
Interior Design: Karen Williams [intudesign.net]

Cool Springs Press books may be purchased in bulk for educational, business, fundraising, or sales promotional use. For information, please e-mail **Special Markets@ThomasNelson.com.**

Visit the Cool Springs Web site at **www.CoolSpringsPress.net.**

TABLE OF CONTENTS

CULTURE
& HISTORY   5

TRAVEL   32

WILDLIFE   61

BUSINESS   78

WEATHER   90

SPORTS   122

COOKING   146

GARDENING
& OUTDOORS   174

HI Y'ALL!

THE BOOK YOU HOLD IN YOUR HANDS was created to celebrate everything that is unique and wonderful about that part of the country called "the South." Part geography and part psychology, the South conjures images of lazy summer afternoons on the porch with an ice-cold lemonade, Spanish moss dripping from tree-lined lanes, and the sound of cicadas chirping in the woods at dusk.

And that's the thing: there is no one definition of the South—so this book is chock-full of little tidbits of information and Southern stories, from history both tragic and triumphant and the literature of master storytellers, to the sports we follow so spiritedly and the natural beauty of the land that inspires us. Southerners have a great sense of humor about themselves, so you'll find some of that, too, as well as facts and statistics you may not have known before.

So jump in anywhere—we're sure you'll find something interesting to tell your neighbors!

One note: due to the devastation along the Gulf Coast area created by Hurricane Katrina in the late summer of 2005, some items mentioned here may be in various stages of operation. We've made every effort to confirm that they are open for business, but it never hurts to call ahead to be sure.

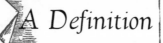

A Definition

Let's get this straight, y'all: we Southerners know what we mean when we refer to the South. That is, there are *Southern* states. And there are states that only *wish* they were Southern! As far as we're concerned, eleven states comprise the South: Alabama, Arkansas, the Carolinas (North and South), Georgia, Kentucky, Louisiana, Mississippi, Tennessee, Virginia, and West Virginia. 'Nuff said.

It's a land that's perfect for agriculture, with a long growing season and plenty of rain, and early European settlers did just that. That landing at Jamestown was only the beginning. Large land grants from English kings who controlled the American colonies ensured an influx of English, Scottish, and Irish immigrants who established large plantations to grow tobacco and cotton; they solved a need for laborers by taking advantage of the slave trade, setting the stage for everything—both tragic and wonderful—that was to follow.

THE OLD SOUTH

Certainly the image of the Old South has been immortalized in books, music, and movies—and after the deplorable dependence on slavery resulted in a civil war that decimated the countryside and changed life on both sides of the Mason-Dixon line for generations, everyone, even Southerners, agreed the old ways had to go.

THE NEW SOUTH

The South has morphed from old to new more than once. The new, post Civil War South ultimately produced a way of life that today we call old: old ways of thinking about folks that manifested in segregation. The Civil Rights movement once again gave us a New South, but in the light of the twenty-first century, those days, too, seem somehow old. Today the South has a vital economy less rooted in agriculture. With manufacturing, high technology, communications, finance, and tourism leading the way, economic success has produced a region rich in diversity. And yet…if you look for it, the best parts of the Old South are still here: strong family ties, southern-style hospitality, and homegrown 'maters!

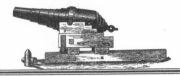

THE SOUTH'S MILTARY HEROES

The South has a strong military tradition (Tennessee even calls itself the "Volunteer State" after the number of volunteer soldiers it contributed to the War of 1812, and every U.S. war thereafter) and is rightfully proud of its heroes.

JOHN PAUL JONES

Although born in Scotland, seaman Jones had immigrated to Virginia when the American colonies revolted against British rule, and the new country was desperate for able maritime commanders. As a lieutenant and later ship's captain in the Continental Navy, Jones was the first to hoist an American flag on an American naval vessel. It was in 1779 that Jones, whose ship, the *Bon Homme Richard*, had engaged the British *HMS Serapis*, uttered those now famous words "I have not yet begun to fight" when it appeared that he was outgunned and outmanned. John Paul Jones is called the founder of the American navy. His remains are in the crypt of the U.S. Naval Academy Chapel in Annapolis, Maryland.

ANDREW JACKSON

Born in the Carolinas, America's seventh president (1829–1837) moved to the Tennessee frontier in 1787 and spent most of his life there. Jackson began his career as a lawyer and politician (he was the first Tennessee congressman, upon statehood in 1790), but made his reputation as a military hero, first in fighting Indians and then with his Tennessee volunteers of the War of 1812 (and more particularly of the Battle of New Orleans in 1815), where he earned his nickname "Old Hickory," a result of his reputation for toughness. Assigned to the Florida territory by President Monroe, Jackson's military actions against the Seminoles ultimately caused Spain to cede control to the U.S.

Andrew Jackson

THOMAS JONATHAN (STONEWALL) JACKSON

Born in what's now West Virginia, Jackson's early life quickly became tragic. After his father died, his poverty-stricken mother married a man who disliked her children and orphaned them after her death in childbirth. Jackson's education was sporadic—he was mostly self-taught—and this hindered his appointment to the U.S. Military Academy at West Point, where he began literally at the bottom of his class. Here he displayed the determination and perseverance that would mark the rest of his military career, first in the Mexican War. The outbreak of the Civil War found him commanding southern troops, and he earned his nickname during the first battle at Bull Run, for his reputation for not giving ground ("There stands Jackson like a stone wall. Rally behind the

Virginians!"). Although he died in battle, Jackson's legacy is one of a profoundly religious, loving husband and a brilliant, disciplined military tactician.

TUSKEGEE AIRMEN

When Congress enacted legislation to expand the Air Corps in 1939, a flight training program was established at the historically black Tuskegee Institute (now Tuskegee University) in Alabama, even though the U.S. military was at that time segregated and all previous combat pilots had been white. The 99th Pursuit Squadron was formed as an all-black squadron, and peopled with men who learned to fly at Tuskegee Army Air Field. By 1946, these distinguished flyers had flown more than 15,000 sorties, destroyed over 1,000 German aircraft, received hundreds of Air Medals and more then 150 Distinguished Flying Crosses. Their superior combat record did much to quiet the racism still endemic in the U.S. military, though segregation was not officially ended until 1948—thanks in part to the Tuskegee Airmen.

CHARLES (CHUCK) YEAGER

Born poor in West Virginia, Yeager enlisted in the army air corps as soon as he graduated from high school in order to serve in World War II. Early in the war he was shot down over France and escaped to neutral Spain; although Army policy was that no downed pilot should fly over enemy territory again, a personal appeal to General Eisenhower allowed him to fly combat missions again. He distinguished himself through superior flying skills and success as an "ace" (shooting down thirteen enemy aircraft, five in a single day). After the war, Yeager stayed in the military (now the air force), became a test pilot, and is most famous for being the first to break the sound barrier in 1947. He went on to break many speed and altitude records.

ALVIN YORK

The third of eleven children born to hardscrabble farmers in the mountains of east Tennessee, York grew up hunting to help the family eat, and as a result was an expert marksman. Uneducated and a hell-raiser, he experienced a religious conversion—by all accounts sincere and complete—just before being drafted in 1917; his application as a conscientious objector was rejected, and he was sent to France. In late 1918, Corporal York and eight other men captured an active German machine gun and 132 prisoners. Although he was a celebrated American war hero, he remained humble, returning to his Tennessee home to open a school to educate the poor farmers' children in the area. He was never proud of his exploits.

A PROUD TRADITION OF MILITARY COLLEGES

THE CITADEL,
Charleston, SC
Founded in 1842

NORTH GEORGIA COLLEGE
& STATE UNIVERSITY,
Dahlonega, GA
Founded in 1873

VIRGINIA MILITARY INSTITUTE,
LEXINGTON, VA
Founded in 1839

VIRGINIA TECH
Blacksburg, VA
Founded in 1872

VIRGINIA WOMEN'S INSTITUTE FOR
LEADERSHIP AT MARY BALDWIN
COLLEGE,
Staunton, VA
Founded in 1995

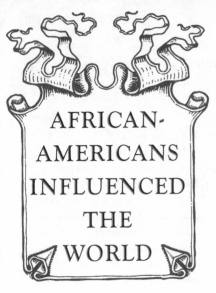

AFRICAN-AMERICANS INFLUENCED THE WORLD

From difficult beginnings came many good things. These African-Americans made a difference in the South—and in the world.

BOOKER T. WASHINGTON (1856–1915)

Born into slavery in Virginia, Washington gained freedom at the end of the Civil War, and moved with his family to West Virginia. There he worked menial jobs so he could attend school, until at age sixteen he walked the 500 miles back to Virginia to attend the Hampton Normal and Agricultural Institute, which had been established to train black teachers. After graduation, he taught first at Hampton, then was recommended for a job at a new normal school in Alabama. Washington became the first principal at Tuskegee Normal and Industrial Institute, and stayed there until his death. He became a popular spokesman for African-Americans, although his efforts to cooperate with whites were later criticized.

Booker T. Washington

GEORGE WASHINGTON CARVER (1864–1943)

Although not born a Southerner—he was born into bondage in Missouri—Carver spent the majority of his career at what is now Tuskegee University in Alabama, using his degrees in botany to improve the lives of poor Southern farmers. It was at Tuskegee that he developed the idea of crop rotation, introducing new crops such as peanuts and sweet potatoes that put nitrogen and other nutrients back into a soil depleted from years of growing cotton. This revolutionary idea—which Carver disseminated by developing an agricultural extension service to train farmers—literally changed lives across a South still struggling to recover from the Civil War. In order to make the new crops profitable, Carver experimented with uses for them; he developed over 300 ways to use peanuts alone (although not, contrary to popular belief, peanut butter). He refused to profit from his many ideas, and helped anyone who asked.

George Washington Carver

W. C. HANDY (1873–1958)

William Christopher Handy was born to former slaves and grew up in Florence, Alabama, in a log cabin built by his grandfather. Although he possessed a keen interest in music, the playing of musical instruments was frowned upon by his preacher father and church, so his ultimate musical success might be called miraculous. After being trained as a teacher, he discovered he could make more money playing in a band, and toured for several years before settling the band on Beale Street in Memphis, where he developed the style of playing we now call 12-bar blues. His composition, "Memphis Blues," is considered the first published blues, and Handy himself is called the "Father of the Blues."

MARY McLEOD BETHUNE (1875–1955)

Born to former slaves in South Carolina, Bethune was the fifteenth of seventeen children; she helped her parents on the family farm and didn't even begin school until she was eleven. But schooling agreed with her, and she persisted to eventually become a teacher herself. Recognizing her good fortune in gaining a formal education, Bethune opened the Daytona Normal and Industrial Institute for Negro Girls (later Bethune-Cookman College), even admitting girls whose parents could not afford the tuition, because she believed that education was the way for African-Americans to achieve equality in this country. She was also active in politics and worked tirelessly to eliminate discrimination and promote interracial cooperation.

WILMA RUDOLPH (1940–1994)

Wilma Rudolph was born prematurely into a large family in Clarksville, Tennessee, and was nursed through a litany of childhood illnesses, including scarlet fever and pneumonia. Diagnosed with polio at age six, the doctors told her parents she'd never walk again, but daily massages and encouragement from her family helped her regain the use of her leg by age twelve, when the tall girl began playing basketball in junior high school. Here she was spotted by Ed Temple, the renowned

Wilma Rucolph

coach of the Tennessee State University women's track team, the Tigerbells, and invited to participate in a Summer sports camp. Rudolph received a full scholarship to TSU, and under Temple's guidance became a world-class runner. In the 1960 Summer Olympics in Rome, she won three gold medals (100 meter, 200 meters, and 4 x 100 meter relay). She went on to graduate from TSU and became a teacher and track coach.

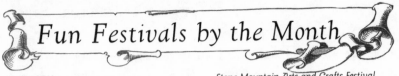

Fun Festivals by the Month

FEBRUARY
Southeastern Flower Show
Atlanta, GA (404) 351-1074

MARCH
Cherry Blossom Festival
Macon, GA (478) 751-7429

SpringFest
Hilton Head, SC (843) 686-4944

St. Patrick's Day Parade and Celebration
Savannah, GA (912) 233-4804

APRIL
New Orleans Jazz and Heritage Festival
New Orleans, LA (504) 558-6100

Fayetteville Dogwood Festival
Fayetteville, NC (910) 323-1934

Main Street Festival
Franklin, TN (615) 591-8500

MerleFest (Americana Music Celebration)
Wilkesboro, NC (336) 838-6100

MAY
Antique Alley Yard Sale
(502 miles on Hwy 11, from Meridian, MS
to Bristol, VA) (877) 871-1386

Atlanta Jazz Festival
Atlanta, GA (404) 853-4234

Mudbug Madness
Shreveport, LA (318) 222-7403)

Shenandoah Apple Blossom Festival
Winchester, VA (540) 722-8700

Memphis in May
Memphis, TN (901) 525-4611

Beale Street Spring Music Festival
Memphis, TN (901) 525-4611

Sweet Auburn Springfest
Atlanta, GA (404) 886-4469

Tennessee Renaissance Festival
Triune, TN (615) 395-9950

Savannah College of Art and Design
Sand Arts Festival
Tybee Island, GA (912) 525-6701

JUNE
Spoleto Festival
Charleston, SC (843) 722-2764

Fiddlers' Jamboree and Craft Show
Smithville, TN (615) 597-8500

Stone Mountain Arts and Crafts Festival
Stone Mountain, GA (404) 925-7056

JULY
W.C. Handy Music Festival
Muscle Shoals Area, AL (256) 766-7642

Bele Chere Festival
Asheville, NC (828) 259-5800

AUGUST
Kentucky State Fair
Louisville, KY (502) 367-5180

West Virginia State Fair
Lewisburg, WV (304) 645-1090

Original Southwest Louisiana Zydeco
Music Festival
Opelousas, LA (337) 942-2392

SEPTEMBER
Tennessee State Fair
Nashville, TN (615) 862-8980

Virginia State Fair
Richmond, VA (800) 588-3247

Georgia State Fair
Macon, GA (478) 746-7184

OCTOBER
Alabama National Fair
Montgomery, AL (334) 272-6831

Newport Autumn Art Fest
Newport, KY (513) 297-1573

October Court Day
Mount Sterling, KY (866) 415-7439

Webb School Arts and Crafts Fair
Bell Buckle, TN (931) 389-9663

Southern Festival of Books
Nashville, TN (615) 770-0006

Louisiana State Fair
Shreveport, LA (318) 635-1361

Mississippi State Fair
Jackson, MS (601) 961-4000

North Carolina State Fair
Raleigh, NC (919) 821-7400

South Carolina State Fair
Columbia, SC (803) 799-1760

NOVEMBER
Natchez Fall Arts, Crafts & Gifts Show
Natchez, MS (318) 336-5572

Mountaineer Week
Morgantown, WV (304) 293-2702

FATHER OF THE BILL OF RIGHTS
JAMES MADISON

Virginian James Madison attended the College of New Jersey (which later became Princeton University) and shortly thereafter served in the Virginia state legislature, where he became a protégé of Thomas Jefferson. Madison was a delegate to the Continental Congress, and was the primary author of the U.S. Constitution, as well as a staunch leader in the campaign to ratify it... but his role in the creation of the Bill of Rights is less well known.

You see, although we now consider these amendments vitally important, back then delegates were divided in their opinions about their effectiveness.

Madison, in fact, did not believe a bill of rights necessary (although he was also not opposed), but he saw that opinion was strong for adding it and that the lack of one was impeding ratification of the Constitution—and he was enough of a politician to feel compelled to take charge of the process. Against opposition, Madison succeeded in presenting a bill of rights on June 8, 1789, and eventually ten amendments were adopted, which we now call the Bill of Rights. You could say Madison was a freedom fighter.

1. Freedom of speech, press, religion, peaceable assembly, and to petition the government.
2. Right to keep and bear arms.
3. Protection from quartering of troops on private property.
4. Protection from unreasonable search and seizure; warrants shall be for specific probable cause.
5. Right to due process; no double jeopardy or self-incrimination; no seizure of private property without compensation.
6. Right to a speedy, public trial by jury in your own district; to know the nature of the accusation and confront accusers; to compel witness, and to a defense lawyer.
7. Right to a civil trial by jury.
8. Prohibition of excessive bail, as well as cruel or unusual punishment.
9. Protection of rights not specifically listed in the Bill of Rights.
10. Powers not delegated to the federal government reside with states and the people.

CAN YOU LIST THE BILL OF RIGHTS?

THE SOUTH'S 25 LARGEST CITIES

BATON ROUGE, LA : 227,818

GREENSBORO, NC : 223,891

ATHENS, GA: 201,755

MONTGOMERY, AL: 201,568

SHREVEPORT, LA: 200,145

GREATER ATLANTA, GA: 832,948

NORFOLK/VIRGINIA BEACH, VA: 659,660

MEMPHIS, TN: 650,100

NEW ORLEANS/METAIRIE, LA: 630,810

NASHVILLE, TN: 569,891

CHARLOTTE, NC: 540,828

NEWPORT NEWS/HAMPTON, VA: 326,587

PORTSMOUTH/CHESAPEAKE, VA: 299,749

RALEIGH, NC: 276,093

LEXINGTON, KY: 260,512

LOUISVILLE, KY : 256,231

BIRMINGHAM, AL: 242,820

MOBILE, AL: 198,915

RICHMOND, VA: 197,790

AUGUSTA, GA: 195,182

ARLINGTON, VA: 189,453

DURHAM, NC: 187,035

COLUMBUS, GA: 186,291

WINSTON-SALEM, NC: 185,776

JACKSON, MS: 184,256

The Capitol Building in Atlanta, Georgia.

*FROM THE U.S. CENSUS BUREAU 2000

Murder of King Cotton!

IN THE SOUTH, cotton was king...until King Cotton was murdered by a tiny bug: the boll weevil (*Anthonomus grandis*). In an infestation moving north from Mexico, the boll weevil crossed into Texas in 1892 and proceeded to lay waste to cotton fields wherever it found them. You see, the beetle may only be a quarter-inch long, but it has a big appetite for the cotton boll. By 1915 the pest reached southeastern Alabama, South Carolina by 1921, and by the mid-1920s it had entered all cotton growing regions in the South. To this day, it's the most destructive cotton pest in North America.

The timing was terrible: Southern farmers battling the boll weevil were further devastated by the Great Depression. However, the boll weevil changed the face of the South by forcing farmers to diversify crops. In fact, today's peanut farmers—and anyone who loves a good PBJ (not to mention the peanuts-and-Coke favored by Southerners)—owe thanks to the boll weevil. Dr. George Washington Carver had championed the humble legume as a way to improve the lot of poor Southern dirt farmers whose soil had been depleted by repeated cotton crops, and a shift to peanuts and other crops revitalized the rural Southern economy.

WORLD'S ONLY MONUMENT TO A PEST!

In Enterprise, Alabama, at the intersection of College and Main streets, there stands a pedestal surrounded by a lighted water fountain; atop it is a statue of woman in flowing gown, arms stretched over her head ... holding a huge boll weevil. We kid you not. After boll weevils devoured two-thirds of Coffee County's cotton crop in 1915, local farmers were forced to diversify, and the town continued to prosper.

> The mascot of the University of Arkansas–Monticello is the Boll Weevil.

SOUTHERN ZODIAC SIGNS

OKRA (DECEMBER 22 – JANUARY 20)
Okras appear tough and a little prickly on the outside but are really tender characters at heart. Okras have great influence on others, often spreading the seeds of their influence everywhere. And we mean everywhere. Beware Moon Pies!

CHITLIN (JANUARY 21 – FEBRUARY 19)
Chitlins—though they come from humble backgrounds—can make something of themselves if they have lots of seasoning. Chitlins are not very self-aware because what they find is a little disturbing. Chitlins often alienate companions, but go well with Catfish and Okras.

BOLL WEEVIL (FEBRUARY 20 – MARCH 20)
Boll Weevils are extremely curious, often feeling the need to bore deep into the interior of things. You are very intense, as if driven by some inner hunger. Forget about marriage or friends, unless they are wearing cotton.

MOON PIE (MARCH 21 – APRIL 20)
Moon Pies are easy to recognize by their physical appearance—big and round. This might be the year you diet, but it's doubtful. You'll have to sell yourself on your sweet nature. At least try. It won't be easy.

POSSUM (APRIL 21 – MAY 21)
Possums have a natural tendency to withdraw into a don't-bother-me attitude. Sometimes you become so withdrawn you even appear dead. This may be counterproductive. Possums like everyone, but the feeling is not often reciprocated. Check out Armadillos.

CRAWFISH (MAY 22 – JUNE 21)
Crawfish are one of the water signs. You often prefer to hang out in the bathroom. When frightened, your instinct is to run backwards as fast as possible,

and you turn bright red when overheated. Doesn't sound attractive, does it? Still, try meeting a Catfish.

COLLARDS (JUNE 22 – JULY 23)

Collards love to join the melting pot of life and mingle your essence with those around you. Collards make good social workers, psychologists, and professional baseball managers. Stay away from Moon Pies; it won't work. It's just not a good combination.

CATFISH (JULY 24 – AUGUST 23)

Catfish are not easy to understand; even your name is confusing. Most people like Catfish even though you prefer the murky bottoms to the clear surface of life. You might get along well with Okras and Collards—it's worth a try!

GRITS (AUGUST 24 – SEPTEMBER 23)

Grits enjoy being a small part of the larger whole. You especially like to huddle with a big crowd of other Grits. You enjoy all meals but breakfast is your specialty. You get along well with everyone.

BOILED PEANUT (SEPTEMBER 24 – OCTOBER 23)

Despite Boiled Peanuts passionate desire to help mankind, your personality is often too salty. When you come out of your shell, though, you are actually much softer than you appear. Boiled Peanuts go with everyone, especially if they are drinking a cola drink.

BUTTER BEAN (OCTOBER 24 – NOVEMBER 22)

Butter Beans have no enemies, which makes them great party guests. You should be proud that, on the vine of life, you are at home no matter the setting. You can try a relationship with a Chitlin, but we can't guarantee anything.

ARMADILLO (NOVEMBER 23 – DECEMBER 21)

Despite your hard exterior, Armadillos are actually quite soft inside. You're old-fashioned, a throwback to a previous era. Like, virtually prehistoric. You will probably marry another Armadillo but you might want to check out Possums, also.

THE
MASON-DIXON LINE

Although this term has come to signify the psychological division between Yankees and Southerners, it has its roots in an older dispute. It seems that in 1632, King Charles I of England granted some land to Lord Baltimore, in what is now Maryland.

Some fifty years later the second King Charles gave land to William Penn, in what is now, you guessed it, Pennsylvania. Just one problem: the descriptions didn't match, and in 1750 the two families took the case to a British court for a decision. A decade later a compromise was reached, and all that remained was to have a thorough survey done, so two surveyors were imported from England. Charles Mason and Jeremiah Dixon arrived in Philadelphia in November 1763, and began the difficult job. It took them nearly four years to survey a 233-mile-long line, which promptly became known as the Mason-Dixon line. This boundary played yet another role in history in 1820, when Congress passed the Missouri Compromise, which determined which new states and territories to the west would prohibit slavery. Although the actual Mason-Dixon survey only divided Pennsylvania from Maryland, this boundary was extended, and ultimately gave its name to the line that geographically divides Northern states from Southern states.

Conceived as an American folk opera and set in Charleston, SC, *Porgy and Bess* contributed several songs to popular Southern culture, including "I Got Plenty o'Nuttin'," "It Ain't Necessarily So," and the oft-covered "Summertime." Although composer George Gershwin and co-lyricist Ira Gershwin were New Yorkers, DuBose Heyward, writer of the 1924 novel *Porgy*, hailed from Charleston, S.C.

SOUTHERN STATES NICKNAMES

ALABAMA	Yellowhammer State
ARKANSAS	The Natural State
GEORGIA	The Peach State
KENTUCKY	The Bluegrass State
LOUISIANA	The Pelican State
MISSISSIPPI	The Magnolia State
NORTH CAROLINA	The Tar Heel State
SOUTH CAROLINA	The Palmetto State
TENNESSEE	The Volunteer State
VIRGINIA	The Old Dominion State
WEST VIRGINIA	The Mountain State

The Southern Belle

A SOUTHERN BELLE...

- Always remembers to act like a lady—no matter what.
- Knows there's no substitute for good manners and no excuse for bad ones.
- Always says "Ma'am" and "Sir" when speaking to her elders.
- Understands that it is never too soon to write a thank-you note.
- Expects her door to be opened and her chair to be held.
- Loves to flirt, although she wouldn't be caught dead chasing a man!
- Refers to all men as gentlemen, except her father, who will always be "Daddy."
- Calls everyone else "Darlin'," "Honey," or "Sweetie."
- Believes that the country club is her second home.
- Makes sure that her pearls and silver are real.
- Always looks her best.
- Would never leave the house without makeup and, ahem, the proper foundation undergarments.
- Doesn't sweat; she perspires.
- Never wears white before Easter or after Labor Day—unless she is a bride.
- Knows that certain occasions call for a hat.
- Will not have a gray hair on her head until she's good and ready to.
- Recognizes that food is love, and that the perfect biscuit is better than a kiss.
- Never loses her composure in the face of disaster or tragedy.
- Can be counted on to bail you out of jail, even at 3:00 a.m.
- Recognizes that being a belle takes a lifetime of practice.

THE SOUTHERN GENTLEMAN

A SOUTHERN GENTLEMAN...

- Always opens doors and carries heavy things.
- Is courteous; he remembers the Golden Rule and uses it.
- Immediately removes his hat indoors or when the American flag is displayed.
- Is humble and defers to others.
- Knows that modesty is a virtue; he does not brag, ever.
- Understands that respect is earned, and behaves as if he's trying to earn yours.
- Believes that giving his word means something; he always honors a handshake deal.
- Takes care of personal hygiene.
- Knows how to make a proper introduction.
- Is friendly, sociable, and neighborly; he always smiles.
- Always uses "Ma'am" and "Sir" when speaking to others.
- Never fails to use "please" and "thank you."
- Can be counted on to offer a toast or say a prayer in public—at a moment's notice.
- Is responsible: he shows up when he says he will and does what he's promised to do.
- Takes care of anyone who is dependent on him (wives, children, aged parents, animals).
- Always calls his mother "Momma" or "Mother."
- Refers to women as "ladies" and treats them as if they are royalty since, in the South, they are.
- Never swears in front of ladies.
- Never, never kisses and tells.
- Knows that chivalry is not dead: he stands when a lady enters the room and walks on the outside when accompanying a lady.
- Calls women younger than himself "Miss" (Miss Katie).
- Behaves himself in public and is never loud or uncouth—not even at Neyland Stadium when the Vols are up by three touchdowns.

THE FIGHT FOR CIVIL RIGHTS

Although Lincoln's Emancipation Proclamation (January 3, 1863) theoretically freed slaves living in the South, the struggle for equality remains today. Here are some notable Southerners who have carried on the fight.

Mary Church Terrell (1863–1954)
Writer and civil rights activist Mary Church Terrell was born in Memphis, Tennessee, to a wealthy family. She was one of the first African-American women to earn a college degree and she began her career as a high school teacher and principal. She crusaded against segregation in the Washington D.C. area. She was a founding member of the NAACP, and the first black woman in the United States to be appointed to a board of education.

Rosa Parks (1913–2005)

Called the "Mother of the American Civil Rights Movement," Parks was born in Tuskegee, Alabama. Encouraged by her family and later her husband, Parks completed a high school degree at a time when only 7 percent of African-Americans had a high school diploma. In 1955, she was a working woman on her way home, sitting in the "black section" of a Montgomery bus, when the driver demanded that she give up her seat to a white man. Her refusal—an act of civil disobedience—launched the Montgomery Bus Boycott and the career of Martin Luther King Jr.

Rosa Parks

Martin Luther King Jr. (1929–1968)
Born a preacher's son in Atlanta, Georgia, King was a young preacher himself in Montgomery, Alabama, when Rosa Parks refused to give up her seat on a Montgomery bus. Employing the nonviolent tactics that he would become known for, King organized a boycott of the Montgomery bus system that lasted over a year and successfully ended racial segregation on intrastate buses. A powerful orator, King was awarded the Nobel Peace Prize in 1964 for his efforts to advance racial equality and dignity. King was assassinated in 1968.

Morris Dees (1936-)
Upon graduation from the University of Alabama Law School, Dees founded a successful law firm and book publishing company (eventually one of the largest in the South), and was not particularly involved in the Civil Rights movement. A personal epiphany changed his heart, and he began taking cases that were unpopular in the white community, pursuing equal justice for minorities and the poor. In 1971, he and his law partner opened the Southern Poverty Law Center, a nonprofit law firm dedicated to cases involving civil rights. Dees is most famous for winning landmark cases against hate groups.

"I HAVE A DREAM"

"Let us not wallow in the valley of despair. I say to you today, my friends, that in spite of the difficulties and frustrations of the moment, I still have a dream. It is a dream deeply rooted in the American dream.

"I have a dream that one day this nation will rise up and live out the true meaning of its creed: 'We hold these truths to be self-evident: that all men are created equal.'

"I have a dream that one day on the red hills of Georgia the sons of former slaves and the sons of former slaveowners will be able to sit down together at a table of brotherhood.

"I have a dream that one day even the state of Mississippi, a desert state, sweltering with the heat of injustice and oppression, will be transformed into an oasis of freedom and justice.

"I have a dream that my four children will one day live in a nation where they will not be judged by the color of their skin but by the content of their character.

"I have a dream today ...

"This will be the day when all of God's children will be able to sing with a new meaning, 'My country, 'tis of thee, sweet land of liberty, of thee I sing. Land where my fathers died, land of the pilgrim's pride, from every mountainside, let freedom ring.'

"And if America is to be a great nation this must become true. So let freedom ring from the prodigious hilltops of New Hampshire. Let freedom ring from the mighty mountains of New York. Let freedom ring from the heightening Alleghenies of Pennsylvania! Let freedom ring from the snow-capped Rockies of Colorado! Let freedom ring from the curvaceous peaks of California!

"But not only that; let freedom ring from Stone Mountain of Georgia! Let freedom ring from Lookout Mountain of Tennessee! Let freedom ring from every hill and every molehill of Mississippi. From every mountainside, let freedom ring.

"When we let freedom ring, when we let it ring from every village and every hamlet, from every state and every city, we will be able to speed up that day when all of God's children, black men and white men, Jews and Gentiles, Protestants and Catholics, will be able to join hands and sing in the words of the old Negro spiritual, 'Free at last! Free at last! Thank God Almighty, we are free at last!'"

—MARTIN LUTHER KING, JR.
Keynote address at the March on Washington, August 28, 1963

A Sampler of Southern Music

Don't just think country when you think of the South! After all, the South is also the birthplace of several uniquely American original musical art forms: jazz, blues, and rock-and-roll. Read on, and see what else the South has in store!

BLUES

Based on a specific scale, the blues developed in communities of former African slaves, and was derived from traditional chants and field songs. Occasionally raunchy, blues songs often tell a personal tale of woe.
Be sure to listen to: Charlie Patton, B. B. King, Robert Johnson, Muddy Waters, Buddy Guy, Bessie Smith, John Mayall and the Bluesbreakers, W. C. Handy

BLUEGRASS

Also considered an American art form, bluegrass has its roots in English, Scottish, and Irish traditional music, introduced by immigrants who often settled in Appalachia. As in jazz, various instruments (often mandolin, fiddle, banjo, guitar) switch off the lead melody.
Be sure to listen to: Bill Monroe and His Blue Grass Boys, Flatt and Scruggs, Ricky Skaggs, New Grass Revival, Alison Krause and Union Station, Vassar Clements

COUNTRY

A style of music that developed in the South in the 1920s, country is now a catch-all phrase that encompasses everything from the Nashville sound to honky-tonk. Country songs often relate stories of ordinary life. *Be sure to listen to:* Jimmie Rodgers, Hank Williams, Patsy Cline, Merle Haggard, Johnny Cash, George Jones, Tammy Wynette, Dwight Yoakam, Vince Gill, Lyle Lovett, Keith Urban

GOSPEL

Gospel refers both to music that came out of black churches of the 1930s, with songs often based on old slave spirituals, and the male vocal quartet singing inspirational songs which sprang up in the early 1900s, known as Southern gospel. *Be sure to listen to:* Gaither Vocal Band, the Martins, the Jordanaires, Al Green, Mahalia Jackson, the Five Blind Boys of Mississippi

JAZZ

Another original American art form that originated in New Orleans, although it uses Western music technique and theory, jazz is characterized by unique rhythms and improvisation. There are now many forms of jazz, ranging from Dixieland to Big Band, swing, be-bop, fusion, and even Latin jazz.

Be sure to listen to: Wynton Marsalis, Duke Ellington, Louis Armstrong, Bix Biederbecke, Ella Fitzgerald, Billie Holliday, Charlie Parker, John Coltrane, Miles Davis, Harry Connick Jr., Chick Corea

RAGTIME

Ragtime was developed by itinerant pianists traveling throughout the Mississippi Valley in the late 1890s, playing in dancehalls and bars. Although the era was largely over by 1917, the music enjoys periodic revivals in popularity, often due to its use in movie soundtracks.

Be sure to listen to: Scott Joplin, Jelly Roll Morton

RHYTHM-AND-BLUES/R&B

A term developed in the 1940s to describe popular music performed by African Americans, R&B has now come to encompass funk and soul music as well.

Be sure to listen to: Fats Domino, Ray Charles, James Brown, Aretha Franklin, Sly and the Family Stone, Luther Vandross, Smokey Robinson, Sam Cooke

SOUTHERN ROCK

Played with electric instruments, rock-and-roll combined elements of earlier music types—boogie-woogie, jazz, blues, and others— and emerged in the American South in the 1950s. Southern rock is a distinctive subset, performed by artists distinctly Southern in outlook.

Be sure to listen to: Elvis Presley, Little Richard, Jerry Lee Lewis, the Allman Brothers, Lynyrd Skynyrd, Jimmy Buffett

ZYDECO/CAJUN

Rooted in the French-Canadian ballads, Cajun music is often performed alongside zydeco, which has its basis in a Creole heritage. Instruments used in clued fiddle, accordian, and the triangle.

Be sure to listen to: Clifton Chenier, Jo-El Sonnier, Beausoleil, Zachary Richard, Jimmy C. Newman, Doug Kershaw, Rockin' Sidney, Buckwheat Zydeco, Boozoo Chavis

*"My version of 'Georgia' became the state song of Georgia.
That was a big thing for me, man. It really touched me. Here is a
state that used to lynch people like me suddenly declaring my version of a song as its state song. That is touching."*

—RAY CHARLES

We Can Dance, Too!

BLACK BOTTOM
Originated in New Orleans in the early 1900s.

CAJUN JIG
Danced with a partner, and utilizes
a single, limping step.

CAROLINA SHAG
Evolved from dances of the Big Band era,
originally at Myrtle Beach, South Carolina.

CHARLESTON
Named for the South Carolina city, a popular
dance craze of the 1920s.

CLOGGING
Originated in Appalachia (although brought from Europe), a type of
percussive dance characterized by stomping and other footwork.

SQUARE DANCE
Danced with four couples to specific patterns called out by a caller;
originated in Europe and immigrated to the U.S.

VIRGINIA REEL
Folk dance dating from the seventeeth century; most famously
performed in *Gone With the Wind*.

WANT TO HEAR MORE?

MUSICOLOGIST JOHN LOMAX (LATER FOLLOWED BY HIS SON,
ALAN) SPENT YEARS IN THE SOUTH, RECORDING AND
PRESERVING SONGS FOR THE LIBRARY OF CONGRESS. MANY OF
THESE FIELD RECORDINGS ARE AVAILABLE COMMERCIALLY.
CHECK THEM OUT!

THE WRIGHT STUFF

December 17, 1903. A bitterly cold wind blew in off the Atlantic, and whipped sand across the lonely beach at Kitty Hawk, North Carolina. South of the township, at Kill Devil Hills, Brothers Wilbur and Orville Wright, fascinated by flight from their youth, were ready to make their first attempt at manned, controlled flight.

Several years of experimenting resulted in the 1903 Flyer that stood on this windswept stretch of land, a biplane built of spruce and ash and French sateen cloth, powered by a four-cylinder, 12 hp gasoline engine and two propellers. Its unmanned weight was 605 pounds, wingspan 40ft. 4in., and length from nose to tail 21ft. 1in.

Orville Wright

The brothers had flipped a coin to see who would go first, and Orville won the toss. "With a short dash down the runway, the machine lifted into the air and was flying. It was only a flight of twelve seconds, and it was an uncertain, wavy, creeping sort of flight at best," wrote Orville, "but it was a real flight at last and not a glide."

The airplane had covered a mere 120 feet, but it was a start.

And the rest, as they say, is history.

Wilbur Wright

The United States Patent Office granted the Wright brothers a patent for their "Flying Machine" on May 22, 1906. The scientific principles in the patent are the basis for the design of all airplanes that have been made since.

U.S. PRESIDENTS...

George Washington	Born in Westmoreland Co., VA
Thomas Jefferson	Born in Shadwell, VA
James Madison	Born in Port Conway, VA
James Monroe	Born in Westmoreland Co., VA
Andrew Jackson	Born in Waxhaw, SC
William H. Harrison	Born in Berkeley, VA
John Tyler	Born in Greenway, VA
James Knox Polk	Born in Mecklenburg Co., NC
Zachary Taylor	Born near Barboursville, VA
Abraham Lincoln	Born in Hardin (now Larue) Co., KY
Andrew Johnson	Born in Raleigh, NC
Woodrow Wilson	Born in Staunton, VA
James Earl Carter, Jr.	Born in Plains, GA
William Jefferson Clinton	Born in Hope, AR

SOUTHERNERS ALL!

WHAT'S A DIXIECRAT?

It's the term first used to describe supporters of Strom Thurmond's 1948 third-party candidacy for U.S. president.

LIFE, LIBERTY, AND THE PURSUIT OF HAPPINESS

Southerners have long been known as powerful orators and writers. Virginian Thomas Jefferson is one of the best known, for good reason—he was the author of the Declaration of Independence. Here is an excerpt of that document.

Thomas Jefferson

We hold these truths to be self-evident, that all men are created equal, that they are endowed by their Creator with certain unalienable rights, that among these are life, liberty and the pursuit of happiness. That to secure these rights, governments are instituted among men, deriving their just powers from the consent of the governed. That whenever any form of government becomes destructive to these ends, it is the right of the people to alter or to abolish it, and to institute new government, laying its foundation on such principles and organizing is powers in such form, as to them shall seem likely to effect their safety and happiness. Prudence, indeed, will dictate that governments long established should not be changed for light and transient causes; and accordingly all experience hath shown that mankind are more disposed to suffer, while evils are sufferable, than to right themselves by abolishing the forms to which they are accustomed. But when a train of abuses and usurpations, pursuing invariably the same object evinces a design to reduce them under absolute despotism, it is their right, it is their duty, to throw off such government, and to provide new guards for their future security.

Southern Literary GIANTS

What is it about the South that it has produced so many literary masterpieces? We don't know for sure, but these writers established Southern Lit, one of the greatest literary genres of all time.

WILLIAM FAULKNER (1897–1962)
The Sound and the Fury

William Faulkner

Born in Mississippi, Faulkner set many of his stories in fictional Yoknapatawpha County, including this work of genius. Faulkner's tale is of a once-prominent Southern family on the verge of self-destruction, told from four different points of view. Published in 1929, it played a significant role in Faulkner's winning the Nobel Prize for Literature in 1949.

MARGARET MITCHELL (1900–1949) *Gone With the Wind*

Atlanta native Mitchell was ten years old before she learned the South had lost the War, having grown up surrounded by relatives who'd survived it. She used their stories and details from her own life to write her blockbuster, which won the Pulitzer Prize in 1937. It has sold more copies than any other hardcover book except the Bible.

JAMES AGEE (1909–1955) *A Death in the Family*

Tennessean Agee won the Pulitzer Prize in 1958 for this semiautobiographical work about a happy family destroyed by the death of the father, told through the eyes of a six-year-old. Poetic, musical prose temper the grim subject.

TENNESSEE WILLIAMS (1911–1983) *A Streetcar Named Desire*

Williams's story about an aging Southern belle won the Pulitzer Prize for drama in 1948, and is one of the most heartbreaking stories about men's expectations of women ever written. Williams was born in Mississippi but lived much of his life in New Orleans, where *Streetcar* is placed.

HARPER LEE (1926–) *To Kill a Mockingbird*

Told through the eyes of a child, Harper Lee's story about race, class, and injustice was an immediate bestseller when it was published in 1960 (it won the

Pulitzer Prize for Fiction in 1961). Lee, a native of Alabama, was a childhood friend and neighbor of Truman Capote. She has not published another novel.

LEE SMITH (1944–) *Fair and Tender Ladies*
Smith grew up in the Appalachian hills of Virginia, and almost all her novels pay homage to the people and geography of this isolated area, including *Ladies*. Told in letters—and quaint dialect of the early twentieth-century South—this beloved novel won the Sir Walter Raleigh Award in 1989 and played a part in Smith's winning the Robert Penn Warren Prize for Fiction in 1991.

KAYE GIBBONS (1960–) *Ellen Foster*
North Carolinian Gibbons writes honestly about her Southern characters, never pitying their hardships. This first novel was recently honored in London as one of the Twenty Greatest Novels of the Twentieth Century, and has become a classic taught in high school and college literature classes.

MIDNIGHT IN SAVANNAH

When *Midnight in the Garden of Good and Evil*, John Berendt's exposé about the events surrounding a real-life local murder trial, was published in 1994, it became an overnight bestseller... but Savannah locals were of mixed feelings about it. On the one hand, the city of Savannah stunningly lives and breathes in the pages of Berendt's slightly fictionalized nonfiction book, and has brought hundreds of thousands of new tourists to the city. On the other, of course, there are some less-than-flattering portrayals of, well, real people. Over a decade later "The Book" has resulted in trolley and cemetery tours, memorabilia shops, guidebooks, and endless conversation.

Want to see it for yourself? Here are two tours that will show you all the sights!
• Gray Line Tours: Savannah, 215 W. Boundary St., (800) 426-2318
• The Book Gift Shop: Savannah, 127 E. Gordon Sq., (912) 233-3867

My mother, Southern to the bone, once told me, "All Southern literature can be summed up in these words: 'On the night the hogs ate Willie, Mama died when she heard what Daddy did to sister.'"

—*PAT CONROY*

Don't Miss These!
30 of the Best Southern Novels

Most Southern literature has a few common elements, such as the importance of family (odd as it may be), community (odd as it may be), and spirituality (odd as it may be), as well as history, race issues, and dialect. While there are many, many great Southern books, we recommend the following to get you started …

James Lee Burke *In the Electric Mist with Confederate Dead*

Erskine Caldwell *Tobacco Road*

Truman Capote *Other Voices, Other Rooms*

Pat Conroy *Prince of Tides*

James Dickey *Deliverance*

Clyde Edgerton *Walking Across Egypt*

Fannie Flagg *Fried Green Tomatoes at the Whistle Stop Café*

Charles Frazier *Cold Mountain*

Ernest Gaines *The Autobiography of Miss Jane Pittman*

Ellen Gilchrist *Victory over Japan*

Alex Haley *Roots*

Josephine Humphreys *Dreams of Sleep*

Zora Neale Hurston *Their Eyes Were Watching God*

Carson McCullers *The Member of the Wedding*

Willie Morris *North Toward Home*

Flannery O'Connor *The Complete Stories*

Walker Percy *The Moviegoer*

Katherine Ann Porter *The Collected Stories*

Padgett Powell *Edisto*

Reynolds Price *Kate Vaiden*

Anne Rivers Siddons *Peachtree Road*

William Styron *The Confessions of Nat Turner*

Peter Taylor *A Summons to Memphis*

Alice Walker *The Color Purple*

Robert Penn Warren *All the King's Men*

Booker T. Washington *Up From Slavery*

Eudora Welty *The Collected Short Stories*

Thomas Wolfe *Look Homeward, Angel*

Richard Wright *Black Boy*

MYSTERIOUS DEATH ON THE NATCHEZ TRACE

The mysterious death of explorer Meriwether Lewis on the Natchez Trace in 1809 has puzzled historians for almost 200 years. Was it murder or suicide?

Soon after President Thomas Jefferson purchased the Louisiana Territory in 1803, he commissioned Captain Meriwether Lewis and William Clark to explore westwards to the Pacific Ocean, to map the American West and study Indian tribes, botany, geology, and wildlife. The Lewis and Clark expedition was a heroic success as the team traveled 8,000 miles in twenty-eight months, the first U.S. overland expedition to the Pacific coast and back.

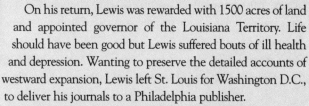
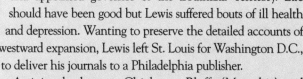

On his return, Lewis was rewarded with 1500 acres of land and appointed governor of the Louisiana Territory. Life should have been good but Lewis suffered bouts of ill health and depression. Wanting to preserve the detailed accounts of westward expansion, Lewis left St. Louis for Washington D.C., to deliver his journals to a Philadelphia publisher.

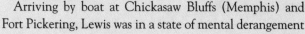

Merriweather Lewis

Arriving by boat at Chickasaw Bluffs (Memphis) and Fort Pickering, Lewis was in a state of mental derangement and had made two attempts at suicide (thwarted by the crew). The fort commandant confined Lewis for two weeks. Altering his plans and heading inland to the Natchez Trace, Lewis separated from his companions and rode alone to a tavern known as Grinder's Stand, just 70 miles from Nashville.

He acted strangely that night, pacing the floor distractedly, talking violently to himself, and showing little appetite. He requested extra gunpowder from his companions, and was heard pacing for many hours until two gunshots split the night. Peering outside and seeing his shadowy figure lurching outside, calling for water, the tavern's owner Mrs. Grinder was afraid to venture out till morning. She found him several hours later in his bed, dying from gunshot wounds to the chest and forehead.

Murder is still suspected by many in the area, but his death was declared a suicide by his companions and President Jefferson. Dr. Reimert Ravenholt, an expert in infectious diseases for the Federal Centers for Disease Control, studied many reports and journals of Lewis and Clark and concludes that Lewis may have suffered from neurosyphilis. Lewis' diary records sexual contact with infected tribes, and the subsequent illness of many of their corps. Lewis' own recurring illness since the expedition fit the symptoms of the disease, which eventually leads to complete and permanent madness, and could provide an explanation for suicide.

Y'all Come Back!

ASHEVILLE, NC

Nestled in the heart of the Blue Ridge Mountains, Asheville has been noted as an ideal place to live in both *Rolling Stone* and *Modern Maturity* magazines! In fact, it's been a popular vacation destination since the 1920s. With a sophisticated arts community, a historic downtown, plenty of outdoors activities, and a pleasant climate—not to mention that big hotel—you'll love your stay in Asheville.

Don't miss: the Biltmore Estate, America's largest home (One Approach Rd., Asheville, NC 28803; (877) 245-8667 or (828) 225-1333)

AUGUSTA, GA

This beautiful Southern city's famed golf tournament tends to overshadow its many other charms, which includes the lovely Riverwalk, dozens of antebellum homes, museums, wildlife preserves, and gardens—not to mention a pleasant year-round climate and plenty of shopping in the historic downtown (Augusta was founded in 1736).

Don't miss: Springfield Baptist Church, the oldest independent African-American congregation in the country (1787). (114 12th St., Augusta, GA 30901; (706) 724-1056)

CHARLESTON, SC

Founded in 1670, subtropical Charleston oozes Southern charm and history—including the Old Exchange and Customs House, and important Colonial-era buildings. With a unique architectural style, and a unique accent strongly influenced by the African-American Gullah community, Charleston's plantations, museums, gardens, churches, and festivals (Spoleto) make it a lovely tourist destination.

St. Michael's Church in Charleston, South Carolina

Don't miss: East Bay Street to Battery Park, historic homes and churches ending in a harborside park.(East Battery and Murray Blvd. at Charleston Harbor, Charleston, SC 29401)

GULF SHORES, AL

While tourists head to Florida beaches, this atmospheric seaside resort is a well-kept local secret—with a gorgeous beach not sheltered by barrier islands. Water activities abound, of course, but there's golfing, biking, parks, spas, museums, and history: a Civil War struggle for control of the harbor here resulted in Admiral David Farragut's immortal words, "Damn the torpedoes; full speed ahead!"

Don't miss: Bon Secour National Wildlife Refuge. (12295 State Hwy 180, Gulf Shores, AL 36542 (251) 540-7720)

LOUISVILLE, KY

Home of the Kentucky Derby, Louisville sits on the Ohio River in the heart of bourbon country. A thoroughly modern city with its roots firmly in the past, Louisville boasts the third largest historic preservation district in the U.S., as well as worldclass museums, and much more. Visitors will have fun learning how to pronounce this city's name like a local!

Don't miss: Churchill Downs Racetrack and Kentucky Derby Museum. (704 Central Ave., Louisville, KY 40208 (502) 636-4400

The Kentucky Derby is held the first Saturday in May

HOT SPRINGS, AR

Hot Springs, Arkansas is the only American city that's situated literally within a national park. Hot Springs derives its name from the thermal springs that emerge from Hot Springs Mountain at a temperature of 143 degrees F. and at a rate of one million gallons per day.

*Don't miss:*Bathhouse Row, consisting of eight turn-of-the-century bathhouses. Contact City of Hot Springs, Hot Springs, AR 71901 (501) 321-6808

MEMPHIS, TN

Sitting on the bluffs overlooking the Mississippi River, Memphis is a place to have a rollicking good time—from Graceland to Beale Street, Mud Island to the Pyramid, a barbeque cook-off to the NBA's Memphis Grizzlies, there's truly something for everyone here.

Memphis sits on bluffs overlooking the Mississippi River

Don't miss: National Civil Rights Museum, based in the Lorraine Motel, where Martin Luther King Jr. was assassinated. (450 Mulberry Street, Memphis, TN 38103 (901) 521-9699)

MYRTLE BEACH, SC

Attracting over 14 million visitors a year, Myrtle Beach is known for its wide, sandy Atlantic Ocean beaches, excellent seafood restaurants, and numerous world-class golf courses. The usual season attractions, shopping, and theme parks, as well as a lively nightlife (the Carolina Shag dance craze originated here in the 1940s), give Myrtle Beach the right combination of sun and fun. *Don't miss:* Huntington Beach State Park (16148 Ocean Hwy., Murrels Inlet, SC 29576 (843) 237-4440)

NATCHEZ, MS

The southern terminus of the Natchez Trace Parkway, this historic town on the Mississippi River has French, Spanish, and Native American roots. And since Sherman somehow missed the town on his March to the Sea, Natchez has more antebellum homes than anywhere else in the U.S. Take a tour!

Natchez, Mississippi has more antebellum homes than anywhere else in the United States

Don't Miss: Grand Village of the Natchez Indians, the political and religious capital of the Natchez tribe of the late 17th century. (400 Jefferson Davis Blvd., Natchez, MS 39120 (601) 446-6502)

NEW BERN, NC

Founded by Swiss explorers in 1710, the seaport town of New Bern is the second oldest city in North Carolina, and is packed with over 150 National Register of Historic Places landmarks—including Bradham's Pharmacy, where Pepsi Cola was first created.

Don't miss: Tryon Palace, the first (1767) permanent capital of the colony of North Carolina. (Corner of George and Pollock Streets, New Bern, NC 28563 (800) 767-1560.)

NEW ORLEANS, LA

N'awlins is a lot more than a party town, and even though Hurricane Katrina laid it low, the Big Easy is open and receiving visitors. Tourist favorites like the French Quarter, St. Charles Avenue, Magazine Street, and the Garden District are all bustling with charm.
Don't miss: Lafayette Cemetery No. 1, established in 1833, with unique above ground tombs. (1400 Washington Ave., New Orleans, LA 70130-5752 (504) 525-3377)

St. Louis Cathedral is the oldest church in New Orelans

NORFOLK, VA

Home to the largest naval base in the world, Norfolk is a part of a large metropolitan area that includes Virginia Beach and Newport News at the mouth of the Elizabeth River. Fish off the pier at the working waterfront, visit one of several historic college campuses, or just wander the pedestrian-friendly streets in the vibrant entertainment district.
Don't miss: Battleship *Wisconsin*, the largest and last battleship ever built by the U.S. Navy. (One Waterside Dr., Norfolk, VA 23510 (757) 322-3108)

VICKSBURG, MS

The site of a Civil War battle in 1863 that gave control of the entire Mississippi River to the Union, Vicksburg has a long history associated with

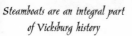

steamboat travel, which has resulted in a rich and diverse local culture. Visitors can enjoy cruises and offshore gaming, as well as museums, historic homes, and gorgeous vistas from the eastern bluffs of the mighty Mississippi.
Don't miss: Vicksburg National Military Park, 16 miles of monuments, cannon, restored gunboat *USS Cairo*, and cemetery. (3201 Clay St., Vicksburg, MS 39183-3495 (601) 636-0583)

Steamboats are an integral part of Vicksburg history

Building a Bridge: The Clinton Library

The William J. Clinton Presidential Library and Museum complex adds a modern flair to the Little Rock, Arkansas landscape. Transforming an urban wasteland into a sculptured landscape, the library is linked with the Clinton Foundation and Clinton School of Public Service to form the new William J. Clinton Presidential Center and Park.

The modern glass and steel building won a National Design Award for excellence in architecture in 2004. Designed by architect James Polchek of Polchek Partnership Architects, New York, the structure cantilevers over the Arkansas River like an elegant metal and glass update of an old rusting railroad bridge. Clinton's famous promise of "building a bridge into the 21st century" takes on new meaning with this second largest presidential library in the United States. The library has three levels and contains 2 million photographs, 80 million pages of documents, 21 million e-mail messages, and nearly 80,000 artifacts from the Clinton presidency. Exhibits include letters to the 42nd President and First Lady from celebrities and world leaders, and rotating personal collections of memorabilia.

The second level displays a fascinating, full-scale replica of the Oval Office, partly arranged by Clinton himself, which gives visitors a sense of the weight of history. Both scholars and tourists alike will find this presidential archive worthy of a visit, discovering many aspects of the Clinton era presidency.

The Library is open Monday through Saturday from 9:00 am to 5:00 pm; Sunday from 1:00 pm to 5:00 pm. Admission ranges from free to $7. The Library is closed New Year's Day, Thanksgiving Day, and Christmas Day. Café 42 (so named because Clinton was the 42nd president), in the basement of the Library features Hillary's famous (or infamous, depending on your persuasion) chocolate chip cookies.

The entrance to the Clinton Library.

William Jefferson Clinton became the first president born after World War II to serve in office. He graduated from Georgetown University, attended Oxford University as a Rhodes scholar, and received a law degree from Yale.

A JOURNEY OF
FIVE MILLION STEPS

The Appalachian Trail is the world's longest continuous hiking trail that is maintained. An American treasure running the length of the Appalachian mountain region—about 2,175 miles—the Trail travels through fourteen states from its southern terminus in Springer Mountain, Georgia to the northern terminus in Katahdin, Maine. Nearly half of the trail is within southern states (Georgia, Tennessee, North Carolina, Virginia, and West Virginia).

Fast Facts:

- The Appalachian Trail was completed in 1937
- Was designated a national scenic trail in 1968 (the nation's first)
- Contains more than 2,000 rare, threatened, sensitive, or endangered species
- Travels through six national parks
- More than 8,000 people have hiked the entire trail
- The lowest elevation is 124 feet; the highest is 6,625!
- The trail has more than 165,000 blazes (markers) along it
- You'd have to walk about five million steps to hike the entire length

Black bears (**Ursus americanus**) are seen all along the Appalachian Trail with the Great Smoky Mountains and Shenandoah National Park as the two most likely locations for contact. Although bear attacks are rare, it's wise to become "bear aware" before setting out on the Trail.

SOUTH OF THE BORDER

If silly puns make you laugh, you've come to the right place. Not that you could have missed it—for more than 200 miles on southbound I-95 you've seen so many signs you're on a first-name basis with Pedro, the Mexican personification of South of the Border. And just over the state line in South Carolina, there it is. With the Sombrero Restaurant, gas station, campground, arcade, fireworks store (and nine others), kiddie rides, indoor miniature golf (the Golf of Mexico), a 300-room motel, and enough garish, politically incorrect plaster statues to keep the kids entertained (including a 97-foot-tall Pedro) for hours, South of the Border has something to tickle every funnybone. It's huge, it's hilarious, it's handy, and it's open 24 hours a day, year-round.

GRACELAND

Let's face it, there's two types of folks who go to Graceland: the longtime Elvis fans (they're the ones carrying flowers to lay on the grave), and everyone else. Elvis Presley's 14-acre estate is a must-see if you're anywhere close to Memphis, and not just because you've heard so much about it. Furnished in '60s decor, the site features custom planes and cars, and dozens of costumes, as well as a thorough tour of the mansion and grounds. It's more moving than you'd think—and the people-watching's not bad either. Across the street at Graceland Plaza you can stock up on Elvis memorabilia in several gift shops, or dine in one of three restaurants.

SEE ROCK CITY

Garnet Carter built the nation's first miniature golf course on top of Lookout Mountain, but that wasn't enough. Oh, no. Once his wife started creating her rock garden, sprinkling it with statues of gnomes imported from Germany, a concept was born and Carter set out to market it. At one

time, over 900 barns in 19 states had "See Rock City" painted on the roof, and Rock City, opened in 1932, became a national tourist destination. It is, shall we say, quintessential, hokey kitsch.

Atop Lookout Mountain.

STONEWALL JACKSON PILGRIMAGE

Sometimes even the most serious things can raise eyebrows in a giggly kind of way. Such is the case with the memorials to Stonewall Jackson, one of the most gifted generals on either side of the Civil War, and, indeed, in U.S. history. At the Chancellorsville Battlefield where Jackson was felled (by friendly

Stonewall Jackson

fire), an obelisk marks the spot; nearby, a marker shows where his arm was amputated in the midst of battle. Jackson died of his wounds eight days later, about 30 miles away in Guinea (there's a Stonewall Jackson Shrine at the site); his body is buried in Lexington's haunted Stonewall Jackson Memorial Cemetery. Well, most of it is: his arm has its own grave and marker on the Ellwood Plantation in the Wilderness Battlefield. Your pilgrimage should also include the Stonewall Jackson House in Lexington, his statue on Monument Avenue in Richmond, and don't forget to take in Georgia's Stone Mountain, where his likeness is carved alongside Robert E. Lee and Jefferson Davis. But wait, there's more—Jackson's horse, Little Sorrel, was a hit at county fairs for years after the War; when he died, he was mounted and presented to VMI, where the horse is still a popular attraction.

The Bell Witch
PROJECT

The Bell Witch is the main character in one of America's great ghost stories—a sinister entity that tormented a Tennessee frontier family in the early 1800s, and even made an unwelcome appearance to President Andrew Jackson.

John Bell, a farmer from North Carolina, settled in northern Robertson County, Tennessee with his wife and family on 320 acres of rich farmland beside the Red River. Inspecting a corn field one day in 1817, Bell encountered a bizarre-looking animal with the body of a dog and head of a rabbit. He fired several shots at the strange animal, but it simply vanished. That evening the Bells began hearing mysterious beating sounds on the walls, which increased with force each night.

As time passed, the family experienced more disturbing visitations. Their bedcovers would be mysteriously pulled off, pillows thrown on to the floor by an invisible force, accompanied by whispering, crying and singing voices like that of a feeble woman. The youngest daughter, Betsy, suffered more violent encounters, as the entity pulled her hair, slapped her face and body, and left deep bruises.

John Bell invited his neighbors to spend the night to witness the strange phenomenon, and that couple also experienced the unseen visitors. Word spread and soon people were coming from far and wide to witness

the manifestations of the "Bell Witch". The wonders it performed convinced even the wildest skeptics, as it would take sugar from bowls, spill milk and eventually carry on conversations, pinch and slap, and laugh at its victims' discomfort.

General Andrew Jackson, later president of the United States, heard of the increasingly terrifying disturbances and made a personal visit with his entourage. Bell's sons had previously fought with Jackson in the Battle of New Orleans, and developed a good rapport with the general. Overnight, one of Jackson's men was stuck with pins and severely beaten by the witch, and by morning the men were begging and pleading to leave the Bell farm.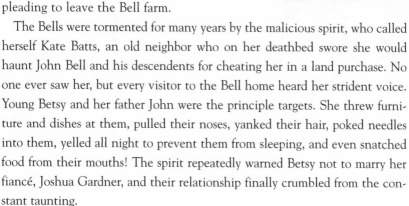

The Bells were tormented for many years by the malicious spirit, who called herself Kate Batts, an old neighbor who on her deathbed swore she would haunt John Bell and his descendents for cheating her in a land purchase. No one ever saw her, but every visitor to the Bell home heard her strident voice. Young Betsy and her father John were the principle targets. She threw furniture and dishes at them, pulled their noses, yanked their hair, poked needles into them, yelled all night to prevent them from sleeping, and even snatched food from their mouths! The spirit repeatedly warned Betsy not to marry her fiancé, Joshua Gardner, and their relationship finally crumbled from the constant taunting.

Under constant attack, John Bell declined in health until his mysterious death by poisoning on December 20, 1820, for which the Bell Witch claimed full credit. The spirit departed several months later with a promise to return in seven years. Sure enough, it came back for a three week visit, then bade farewell after vowing to visit John Bell's most direct descendent in 107 years. Many believe the spirit returned in 1935, and took up residence in Adams, Tennessee, once a part of the Bell farm.

It has been well reported that if you visit the old farm, you may see small lights dancing over the fields, or a mysterious figure in the cave that runs under the farm. If you dare to visit, Adams is located between Clarksville and Nashville, off I-24; follow Highway 76 to Adams. Call ahead (615) 696-3055 for more information. Candlelight tours are available for the brave of heart!

VISITING PARADISE (GARDENS)

Howard Finster, a Baptist preacher from Summerville, Georgia followed an extraordinary path to become America's best-known folk artist. Born into a family of 13 children in Valley Head, Alabama in 1916, Finster had spiritual visions from the age of three. He quit school at 14 and two years later began traveling the tent revival circuit as a preacher. For three decades he traveled throughout Alabama, Georgia, and Tennessee sharing a passion for evangelism.

Exhibiting his unusual creative flair, Finster began a garden park museum in Trion, Georgia, and filled it with his inspired art. He built models of numerous inventions of mankind—houses, churches, duck ponds, bird houses, and made carvings and constructions from scrap objects. Sometimes he painted on plywood or metal, pictures bursting with bright colors, figures surrounded by auras, and jammed with text proclaiming scriptural lessons or observations on life. As a self-taught artist, his style was called "outsider art", meaning, simply, "art from outside the art world." He moved close to Summerville, in northwest Georgia, in 1961 to expand his gardens, which were later dubbed "Paradise Gardens" in an *Esquire* magazine article.

At 60, Finster had a vision that profoundly changed his life. Suddenly seeing a human face on a splash of white paint on his finger, he heard a voice instruct him to paint sacred art. His artworks then became sermons in paint, his way of reaching people to preach the word of God and the message of redemption. He painted relentlessly on anything and everything, numbering each one. God had told him to do 5,000 paintings to spread the gospel, and he was

> Contact (205) 587-3090 or visit www.finster.com/paradisegardens.
> Summerville is about 40 miles from Chattanooga, TN (or about 80 miles from Atlanta).

determined to keep track. Verses of scripture adorned his works and his fame grew.

He appeared on *The Tonight Show* with Johnny Carson and at various folk music festivals; recorded several albums and painted commissioned works for the album covers of R.E.M.'s *Reckoning* and Talking Heads' *Little Creatures*. He made his life a living testimony and used his art to spread the word of God.

Finster died in 2001, having completed over 46,000 pieces of original art. Paradise Gardens remains to preserve his unique art forms, and is open by appointment. The Howard Finster Art Festival takes place in Summerville each May.

GOD BLESS THE TAR HEELS!

Tar, pitch, and turpentine were among North Carolina's major products during the Colonial era. Tar was made by slowly burning wood of the longleaf pine tree, and was used to waterproof ships.

During one of the fierce conflicts of the Civil War, North Carolina troops felt let down by a regiment from another state, when they pulled back from the battle front, weary and despondent.

"Any more tar down in the Old North State, boys?" jibed members of the other regiments.

"Not a bit. Jeff Davis bought it all up," retorted the Carolinians.

"How's that, what's he going to do with it?"

"He's gonna put it on your heels and make you stick better in the next fight," they answered.

Hearing of the incident, General Robert E. Lee remarked "God bless the Tar Heel Boys!" And the nickname has stuck.

Survival Tips for Southerners Moving North

IN CONVERSATION

- The rough translation for "Youse guys" is "Y'all." Can be singular or plural.
- Don't be concerned that you don't understand anyone. They don't understand you either.
- Although you have been taught to say them all your life, permanently remove "Ma'am"and "Sir" from your vocabulary; people will look at you as if you have two heads.
- If you are at a loss for words, just say, "Fuggedaboudit."
- Develop some new small talk; up North, you never need to ask, "Is it cold enough for ya?"
- Every Yankee will think he is better than you. Don't try to correct him; it will only shatter his petty insecurities and jealousies.

INTERPERSONAL RELATIONSHIPS

- A raised middle finger is considered a courteous greeting.
- No waving at passing cars; they think you're simple.
- Be advised that while you may be used to opening doors for ladies, this could be considered a come-on.

CULTURAL ISSUES

- Never ask for grits in a restaurant, and don't expect to find sweet tea anywhere.
- Never, we repeat never, put tomatoes in clam chowder.
- In the North, barbecue is a verb meaning "to cook outside."
- Don't be surprised to find liquor sold in drug stores.
- That spring wardrobe you brought out in April can wait 'til June.
- While you may have been used to doing this all your life, you may never again leave your windows open at night.
- Just because someone is dead doesn't mean he can't vote.

Well, Who Knew?

- West Virginia is the only state in the Union without a natural lake.

- Tennessee and Missouri are bordered by more states than any other! Tennesee is bordered by eight states— Alabama, Arkansas, Georgia, Kentucky, Mississippi, Missouri, North Carolina, and Virginia.

- Scottsboro, Alabama, has the country's largest unclaimed baggage center— a bargain store filled with lost and unclaimed luggage and contents.

- Eleven square miles of Fulton County in southwest Kentucky is cut off from the rest of the state by the Mississippi River. If you wish to travel to this isolated section from the rest of the state, you must first cross a bordering state!

- The University of North Carolina Chapel Hill is the oldest state university in the United States.

- The largest earthquake in American history, the New Madrid Earthquake, occurred in December 1811 in northwestern Tennessee.

- Natchez, Mississippi, has more than 500 buildings on the National Register of Historic Places.

- Several northern parishes (counties) of Louisiana did not support the Confederate cause and, to indicate disapproval, changed their names—Union Parish, Jefferson Parish, Assumption Parish ...

- The New River Gorge Bridge near Fayetteville, West Virginia, is the second highest steel arch bridge in the U.S. and the longest steel arch bridge (1,700 feet) in the world.

The West Virginia quarter features the New River Gorge Bridge.

- North Carolina has the largest state-maintained highway system in the U.S., with 77,400 miles of roads.

- The world's largest cast metal (iron) statue is Vulcan (God of the Forge) in Birmingham, Alabama.

THE MARCH OF THE
Peabody Ducks

Considered one of the South's finest hotels, and the epitome of luxury, elegance, and Southern hospitality, The Peabody has been the social hub of downtown Memphis since it opened in 1869. It is still the place to see and be seen. Presidents, generals, plantation owners, gamblers, and movie stars have crossed the Grand Lobby under the towering hand-painted glass skylights and beautiful carved wooden beams.

George Peabody

The original hotel was built by Colonel Robert C. Brinkley in 1869 and named for the philanthropist George Peabody (who endowed George Peabody College in Nashville). Brinkley gave The Peabody to his daughter as a wedding gift in 1869. The hotel had 75 rooms with private baths, a ballroom, saloon, and lobby, and it cost $3 to $4 a day for a room and meals—extra for a fire and gaslight. In 1923, the original hotel closed but was reopened in 1925, after a massive renovation and relocation to its present site. Blues musicians made their first recordings in rooms at The Peabody and it was also the site of live radio broadcasts in the 1930s and '40s. The Skyway and adjoining Plantation Roof attracted big band dancers and entertainers such as Tommy Dorsey, Paul Whiteman, Harry James, and Smith Ballew.

Today this historic landmark has 449 spacious guestrooms and suites, designed with simple elegance and class. The Peabody is one of the most popular places in Memphis for weddings, balls, and charitable events. The Peabody's signature restaurant, Chez Philippe, continues to generate international acclaim, now blending an Asian influence with its superb French cuisine.

But if you're curious about the "extras on the bill" at The Peabody, read on.

The Peabody ducks waddled into history back in1930 after two friends imbibed a wee bit too much Tennessee sippin' whiskey and decided to play a prank on the hotel guests. Returning empty-handed from a weekend hunting trip in Arkansas, they slipped their live duck decoys (Yes! it was legal at that time) in the hotel's fountain in the Grand Lobby. The guests were delighted, and five Mallard ducks soon became regulars in the ornate fountain. In 1940, Bellman Edward Pembroke, a former circus animal trainer, became the official Peabody Duckmaster, and delivered the ducks from their hotel rooftop home to the fountain each day, teaching them the famous Peabody Duck March. Every morning at 11 a.m., he would lead the ducks down the elevator to the marble fountain in the Peabody Grand Lobby. A red carpet was unrolled and the ducks would march through crowds of admiring spectators to the tune of John Philip Sousa's "King Cotton March." At 5 p.m., they would march back to the elevator to return to their palace on the hotel rooftop. And so it continues today. (Lest you worry about the ducks, their "tour of duty" lasts only 3 months before they are replaced, at which time they retire to a preserve to live out the remainder of their days.)

> *The Peabody Hotel*
> 149 Union Avenue
> Memphis, TN 48103
> (800) 732- 2639
> www.peabodymemphis.com

Size Matters:
The Biltmore Estate

When young aristocrat George W. Vanderbilt visited the scenic mountain town of Asheville in 1888, he so completely fell in love with the area that he decided to create his own winter estate there. As a high-society health retreat in the western Blue Ridge Mountains of North Carolina, Asheville was entering a boom period as the new railroad industry brought money, power, and affluence to the county.

Vanderbilt purchased 125,000 acres (that is not a misprint!), with a dream to create a home like the great working estates of Europe, as well as build an elegant home to showcase his art collection. Emulating his older siblings, who had built opulent mansions in Rhode Island and New York, Vanderbilt commissioned renowned landscape architect Frederick Law Olmstead (of New York's Central Park fame), to design the grounds and gardens. Celebrated architect Richard Morris Hunt designed the house, named Biltmore after the Vanderbilt's Dutch ancestral home of Bilt, and modeled after several sixteenth century French chateaux, with cutting-edge technology that made guests marvel. Vanderbilt enjoyed central heating, electricity, hot and cold running water, a fire alarm, refrigeration, an elevator, swimming pool with underwater lighting, and an indoor bowling alley. The 125,000 square foot house remains the largest privately owned home in the United States. There are 250 rooms, 65 fireplaces, a bowling alley, indoor pool and possibly a partridge in a pear tree.

George Vanderbilt
(Photo: © The Biltmore Co.)

Cornelia and
Edith Vanderbilt
(Photo: © The Biltmore Co.)

The Vanderbilt's only child, a daughter named Cornelia, married John Cecil in 1924, a descendent of Lord Burghley, the Lord Treasurer to Queen Elizabeth I. The Cecils have managed the Biltmore Estate since 1925, and in 1930 opened it to the public to help revitalize Asheville's economy with increased tourism. The dairy barn

*Photo:
© The
Biltmore
Company.*

was remodeled in 1979, and is now a winery for the popular Biltmore Estate label. Some 48,000 vines of European Vitis vinifera grapes thrive on 70 gently sloping acres in the western portion of the estate, producing wines that have earned more than 100 awards in the winery's first decade.

The Biltmore is open year-round, with an extensive calendar of events, which includes concerts, special dinners, wine tastings, photography workshops, horse shows, garden tours—the list goes on and on. There is a special event for each season culminating in spectacular Christmas festivities throughout November and December.

Visit **www.biltmore.com** for more information on events and admission fees. You cannot possibly expect to see America's largest house and grounds in one day, so plan to spend as many as possible!!

The Vanderbilts were well-known for treating their human staff well, but they also treated retired dairy cows well also. The "old ladies", champion Jersey milkers, were retired to box stalls at Sleepy Hollow Farm, where they lived out their days being cared for with all the special attention they deserved.

THE MISSISSIPPI DELTA

Music lovers will want to make a pilgrimage to the cradle of the blues ... the Mississippi Delta. We don't know who said that the Delta "begins in the lobby of the Peabody Hotel and ends on Catfish Row in Vicksburg" but that's as good a description as any. So by all means, go to Memphis and check into the Peabody (be sure you catch the Duck March at 11:00 a.m. and 5:00 p.m.); you can whet your appetite for the blues on Beale Street.

Next, take a drive down the legendary Highway 61 through the rich, flat farmland of this alluvial plain, and head to Clarksdale, Mississippi. It was here—at the crossroads of Highways 49 and 61—that Robert Johnson may or may not have made a deal with the devil. And it is here you will want to visit the Delta Blues Museum, housed in a period 1918 freight depot.

Travel through any of the small towns—Cleveland, Greenville, Yazoo City—and stop in any downtown juke joint to soak up the sound of the blues. Or visit Indianola, the birthplace of B. B. King ... and while you're there, stop in at Club Ebony, where you can see and hear nationally recognized blues acts.

In Greenwood, you can check out Robert Johnson's final resting place—all three of them (no one knows for sure which, if any, is the real one!). And we won't even get into that one over at Mt/ Zion Baptist Church in Morgan City.

What once was Catfish Row in Vicksburg—a seedy neighborhood of beer joints and fish houses along the river-

Steamboats traveling the Mississippi at night.

front— is now being overtaken by shiny new casinos. But now there's a beautiful outdoor space called Catfish Row Art Park, with play areas, fountains, gardens, murals, and exhibits. And that's just the beginning, of course.

THE KENTUCKY BLUEGRASS REGION

The rolling hills around Lexington are perfect for farming ... and raising horses. To enjoy a few days in this beautiful region, start in Lexington, the "Horse Capital of the World." You can bet on the ponies at Keeneland Race Track during racing season, tour some of more than 450 horse farms in the area, or visit the only state park that's also a working horse farm—the Kentucky Horse Park.

With over 1200 acres, the park also features museums, carriage rides, equine presentations, and the grounds of the National Horse Center. There are several pleasant side trips in this area as well. The birthplace of bourbon, the Bluegrass region is home to Woodford Reserve Distillery, as well as the distillers of Ancient Age and Wild Turkey. Visit Ashland, the beloved country estate of Henry Clay. There are several Civil War battle sites nearby. Or spend some time at the Shaker Village of Pleasant Hill. Once a thriving eighteenth- and nineteenth-century religion, the Shaker's belief in celibacy led to the sect's demise (though there are five or six individuals in Maine who call themselves Shakers). The Pleasant Hill settlement was established in 1805 and today the restored community is a National Historic Landmark, offering tours, a living museum, lodging, dining, crafts, and more.

My Old Kentucky Home
WORDS AND MUSIC BY STEPHEN C. FOSTER

The sun shines bright in the old
   Kentucky home
'Tis summer, the people are gay;
The corn top's ripe and the
   meadow's in the bloom,
While the birds make music all the day;
The young folks roll on the little cabin floor,
All merry, all happy, and bright,
By'n by hard times comes a-knocking at the door,
Then my old Kentucky home, good night!
Weep no more, my lady,
Oh weep no more today!
We will sing one song for
the old Kentucky home,
For the old Kentucky home far away.

TURNING UP THE HEAT

There are five salt domes—salt deposits created when
an ancient ocean that once covered Texas, Louisiana,
and Mississippi evaporated—in the otherwise flat wetlands
of south Louisiana. Surrounded by bayous and
swampland, one of them, Avery Island, is just 160
feet high at its tallest point. More important,
it's the home of Tabasco® Sauce.

The chili pepper plant.

When Edmund McIlhenny returned to his Avery
Island plantation after the Civil War, little had
survived except the capsicum pepper plants he'd
planted to use in cooking the local specialties.
Later he created the sauce that many of us can't live without, and the
McIlhenny Co. has been bottling the stuff for 128 years now. Visitors to the
island can tour the factory and while you're there, enjoy the lush tropical gardens and bird sanctuary established by Edward Avery McIlhenny, second son
of Edmund McIlhenny, in 1892. You'll want to spend some time in the 200-
acre Jungle Gardens and Bird City—it changes with the season and always has
something to offer. And don't forget to pick up some Tabasco Sauce to take
home—now available in one-gallon jugs!

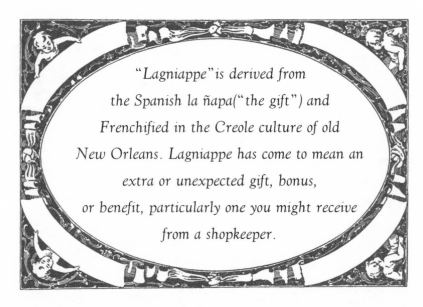

*"Lagniappe"is derived from
the Spanish la ñapa("the gift") and
Frenchified in the Creole culture of old
New Orleans. Lagniappe has come to mean an
extra or unexpected gift, bonus,
or benefit, particularly one you might receive
from a shopkeeper.*

TAKE THE "A" TRAIN... BACK IN TIME

High up in the Monongahela National Forest, where the Alleghenies meet the Appalachians, there's a little piece of history. It's been a long time since steam-driven locomotives were an important method of transportation, but in West Virginia's Cass Scenic Railroad State Park, you can experience what that might have been like. Both the track and the town of Cass were built in 1901 by the West Virginia Pulp and Paper Company to service the then-thriving pulp and logging industry—at one time, the sawmill at Cass was the largest double-band sawmill in the world. Cass was a company town, and today it looks much as it did then. The track, of course, was built to haul lumber from high on Bald Knob Mountain to the mill in Cass.

Alas, the town and the railway were abandoned in 1960, but the state of West Virginia has preserved Cass, a logging camp at Whittaker Station, and Spruce, now a ghost town (thought it was once the coldest and highest town east of the Rockies). Take the two-hour round trip to Whittaker Station, or choose a five-hour round trip to Spruce or to a scenic overlook at Bald Knob.

While you're in the area, fast-forward in time to visit the National Radio Astronomy Observatory in nearby Green Bank, which operates the world's largest fully steerable single aperture antenna telescope. Call 1-800-CALL-WVA, or visit www.cassrailroad.com.

ALL ABOARD!

GEORGIA
- Blue Ridge Scenic Railway
Kentucky
- Bluegrass Railroad Museum
- Big South Fork Scenic Railway
- Kentucky Railway Museum

LOUISIANA
- St. Charles Avenue Streetcar
- Riverfront Streetcar
- Old Hickory Railroad

NORTH CAROLINA
- Charlotte Trolley
- Great Smoky Mountains Railroad
- North Carolina Transportation Museum
- Tweetsie Railroad
- New Hope Valley Railway

TENNESSEE
- Tennessee Central Railroad Museum
- Tennessee Valley Railroad Museum

WEST VIRGINIA
- Cass Scenic Railroad State Park
- Durbin and Greenbrier Valley Railroad
- Potomac Eagle Scenic Railroad

LOOK OUT! NO, LOOKOUT MOUNTAIN ...

It's not really a mountain, it's a plateau. But it just might be one of the prettiest places you've been in awhile—and besides, where else can you be in three states in the same day ... on foot! With its roots in Alabama, Georgia, and Tennessee, this magnificent scenic location offers a sojourn to please everyone.

For the adventurous, the nation's largest hang gliding school (Lookout Mountain Flight Park) offers a tandem hang gliding program that allows folks with no experience at all the opportunity to hang glide with a seasoned veteran.

Outdoor enthusiasts will enjoy Georgia's spectacular Cloudland Canyon State Park, where, frankly, the most impressive view can be had near the picnic area parking lot; however, those who hike to the bottom of the gorge are rewarded with two waterfalls cascading over layers of sandstone and shale into pools below. Need more excitement? The Little River, the nation's longest mountaintop river, flows down the center of Lookout Mountain, and boasts some of the wildest whitewater in the South. The mountain also offers fantastic rock-climbing adventures, caving, and more.

History buffs will want to make a stop at the sobering Chickamauga and Chattanooga National Military Park, where the Battle Above the Clouds (so named due to the fog that settled in the valley below the battlefield) was fought on November 23, 1863.

Finally, after you've taken the kids for a ride on Incline Railway—the world's steepest passenger railway with a slope of 72.7% near the top—there are a variety of inns and B&Bs on the mountain, where you can put your feet up on the porch and watch the sunset.

SEE 7 STATES!

The proprietors of Rock City claim that seven U.S. states can be seen from their vantage point: Tennessee, Kentucky, Virginia, South Carolina, North Carolina, Georgia, and Alabama. But the curvature of the earth's surface actually precludes even the sharpest-eyed tourist from seeing Kentucky, Virginia, and South Carolina—they're simply too far away.

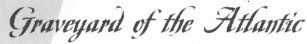

Graveyard of the Atlantic

There aren't many states that offer the dramatic extremes that North Carolina does—from the Great Smoky Mountains in the west to the low-lying Outer Banks on the edge of the Atlantic Ocean and from the sophistication of Charlotte to the laid-back college town of Chapel Hill, visitors can find something interesting to see and do in this scenic state. And we have one suggestion: make a coastal lighthouse pilgrimage!

Make your way to Wilmington, at the mouth of the Cape Fear River, and follow State Route 133 south; there are a couple historic sites along the way, and even though this is a lighthouse tour, we recommend that you take the time to see everything. Oak Island is part of the Coast Guard station and the lighthouse is not open to the public, but you can take pictures. Similarly, Frying Pan Shoals is a platform offshore; you'll need a boat to get close. Bald Head lighthouse is accessible by ferry from Southport, near the junction of 133 and 211, on the mainland.

Price's Creek Lighthouse, along the Cape Fear River, is on private property, but can be viewed from the Fort Fisher / Southport ferry as it approaches the Southport landing. Moving up the coast, make your way to Beaufort and take U.S. 70 east to Harkers Island Road. The Cape Lookout lighthouse is in the Cape Lookout National Seashore. From here, continue on U.S. 70 and then highway 12 to Cedar Island and take the ferry (reservations are recommended) to Ocracoke Island to see the lighthouse there. (Diamond Shoals is a platform offshore.) Continue on 12 to the Cape Hatteras Lighthouse, Bodie Island Lighthouse, and end, finally, at the Currituck Beach Lighthouse

NORTH CAROLINA LIGHTHOUSES

NAME*	SINCE/BUILT	HEIGHT	SIGNAL VISIBLE
Oak Island*	1958 / 1958	169 ft.	19 mi.
Frying Pan Shoals*	1854 / 1964	125 ft.	17 mi.
Bald Head	1817 / 1817	90 ft.	18 mi.
Price's Creek	1848 / 1848	20 ft.	n/a
Cape Lookout*	1812 / 1859	169 ft.	19 mi.
Ocracoke Island*	1803 / 1823	76 ft.	14 mi.
Diamond Shoals	1824 / 1976	175 ft.	20 mi.
Cape Hatteras*	1803 / 1868	225 ft.	20 mi.
Bodie Island*	1847 / 1872	150 ft.	19 mi.
Currituck Beach*	1875 / 1875	162 ft.	19 mi.

With its spiral stripes, the Cape Hatteras Lighthouse is the most recognizable in America. It's also the tallest!

NO DIET FOR FAT TUESDAY

Mardi Gras in New Orleans is an experience most people never forget. A celebration that begins January 6 (Twelfth Night) and continues for two weeks until the beginning of Lent, it is characterized by parades, parties, and general revelry, particularly in the French Quarter. With an international reputation established by 150 years of celebrations, more than 500,000 people annually visit New Orleans during Mardi Gras.

Until Katrina paid a visit. Hurricane Katrina blew through the Louisiana/Mississippi Gulf Coast region on August 29, 2005, leaving a wake of disaster of unheard-of proportions. How would this affect Mardi Gras 2006? After all, in this city of half a million, fewer than half have returned to their homes. The city fathers toyed with the idea of calling the whole thing off.

But that wouldn't be New Orleans! Nope, the krewes wanted to do it. The business owners wanted to do it. And the tourists turned out. There were shrimp po-boys and lemonade and grilled alligator-on-a-stick. There were parades and Mardi Gras beads. There were costumes—one crowd-pleaser was the group dressed as blind men wearing T-shirts that read "Levee Inspectors"—and music blaring in the French Quarter. Approximately 350,000 visitors showed up, and in a city where tourism accounts for 40 percent of revenue, this is an important number. We'll look for you next year!

Visit www.neworleanscvb.com, or call the Convention and Visitors Bureau at 1-800-672-6124.

MARDI GRAS SCHEDULE
Mark your calendar!

2007 – Feb. 20
2008 – Feb. 5
2009 – Feb. 24
2010 – Feb. 16
2011 – Mar. 8
2012 – Feb. 21
2013 – Feb. 12
2014 – Mar. 4
2015 – Feb. 17

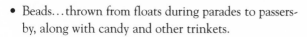

- Balls ... thrown by krewes in the weeks leading up to Mardi Gras Day; most attendees wear elaborate costumes and masks.

- Barkus...an all-dog krewe that parades during Mardi Gras; proceeds benefit the LA/SPCA.

- Beads...thrown from floats during parades to passers-by, along with candy and other trinkets.

- Colors ... purple, green, and gold were first used by the Rex Krewe in 1872, and have come to symbolize Mardi Gras—year-round.

- Indians ... a tradition springing from the African-American community of New Orleans, in which krewes are named after imaginary Indian tribes and participants dress in elaborate Indian costume.

- King cake ... traditionally a cake baked to use up all the lard before Lent. In New Orleans, king cakes come with a plastic baby baked inside: the person who gets the slice with the baby has to buy the next cake—and throw a party!

- Krewe ... coined in 1857, the term refers to any organization that exists to participate in Mardi Gras, generally by raising funds to throw parties and create floats to exhibit in Mardi Gras parades.

MYSTICK KREWE OF COMUS

Founded in 1856, Comus is the oldest continuously active Mardi Gras organization, and is the source of many current New Orleans Mardi Gras traditions, including the term krewe!

KNOWN TRIBES OF THE MARDI GRAS INDIAN NATION

7th Ward Hard Headers	Creole Wild West	Seminole Hunters
7th Ward Hunters	Fi-Yi-Yi	Seminole Skull & Bones
9th Ward Hunters	Flaming Arrows	White Cloud Hunters
Black Eagles	Geronimo Hunters	White Eagles
Black Hawk Hunters	Golden Arrows	Wild Apache
Black Feathers	Golden Blades	Wild Bogacheeta
Black Seminoles	Golden Comanche	Wild Tchoupitoulas
Blackfoot Hunters	Golden Eagles	Wild Magnolias
Carrollton Hunters	Golden Star Hunters	Yellow Pocahontas
Cheyenne Hunters	Guardians of Flames	Young Brave Hunters
Comanche Hunters	Mohawk Hunters	Young Cheyenne
Congo Nation	Morning Star Hunters	Young Monogram Hunters
Creole Osceola	Red Hawk Hunters	Young Navaho

NO MONEY? NO PROBLEM!
Free Things to Do in the South

It's true; some of the best things in life are free! Here are some places to visit that are easy on your wallet. Check with state travel & tourism departments for more ideas.

ALABAMA
- Birmingham Botanical Gardens, Birmingham
- Bon Secour National Wildlife Refuge, Gulf Shores
- Dexter Ave. King Memorial Baptist Church, Montgomery
- Eufala National Wildlife Refuge, Eufala
- Fort Conde, Mobile
- Horsehoe Bend National Military Park, Daviston
- Huntsville Museum of Art, Huntsville
- Little River Canyon National Preserve, Ft. Payne
- Noccalula Falls Park, Gadsden
- Old Cahawba Archaeological State Park, Selma
- Tuskegee Airmen National Historic Site, Tuskegee
- Weeks Bay National Estuarine Research Reserve, Fairhope

ARKANSAS
- Aerospace Education Center, Little Rock
- Arkansas Arts Center, Little Rock
- Beaver Bridge, Beaver
- Boston Mountain Scenic Loop, Mt. Gayler
- Delta Rivers Nature Center, Pine Bluff
- Museum of the Arkansas Grand Prairie, Stuttgart
- The Band Museum, Pine Bluff
- The Old Mill, Little Rock
- Thorncrown Chapel, Eureka Springs
- Wal-Mart Visitors Center, Bentonville
- War Eagle Mill, Rogers
- White Oak Lake State Park, Bluff City

GEORGIA
- A. H. Stephens State Historic Park, Athens
- Bonaventure Cemetery, Savannah
- Cathedral of St. John, Savannah
- Centennial Olympic Park, Atlanta
- Ebenezer Baptist Church, Atlanta
- Fort Augusta/St. Paul's Episcopal Church, Augusta
- Georgia Southern University: Raptor Center, Museum, Botanical Garden, Statesboro
- Martin Luther King Jr. National Historic Site, Atlanta
- Ocmulgee National Monument, Macon
- Phinizy Swamp Nature Park, Augusta
- Piedmont Park, Atlanta
- Riverwalk, Augusta

KENTUCKY
- Boone Station State Historic Site, Athens
- Bourbon distillery tours (Buffalo Trace, Four Roses, Wild Turkey), Lexington
- Covered bridges (Kentucky has 12 remaining), Various locations
- Driving tours of area horse farms, Lexington
- Frankfort Cemetery (Daniel Boone), Frankfort
- Jim Beam Nature Preserve, Nicholasville
- Lexington Cemetery Arboretum and Gardens, Lexington
- Old Governors Mansion (1798), Frankfort
- Outdoor labyrinth at the Old Episcopal Burying Ground, Lexington
- Salato Wildlife Education Center, Frankfort
- Toyota Motor Manufacturing Kentucky, Inc. tour, Georgetown
- University of Kentucky Arboretum, Art Museum, Museum of Anthropology, Lexington

LOUISIANA
- Acadian Cultural Center, Lafayette
- Audubon Park, New Orleans
- Chalmette Battlefield, New Orleans
- Evangeline Oak, Martinville
- Laurens Henry Cohn Sr., Memorial Plant Arboretum, Baton Rouge
- Louisiana State Arboretum, Ville Platte
- LSU: Indian Mounds, Museum of Geoscience, Museum of Natural Science, Union Art Gallery, Baton Rouge
- New Orleans Jazz National Historical Park, New Orleans
- Plaquemine Locks, Baton Rouge
- R. S. Barnwell Memorial Garden and Art Center, Shreveport
- Southern Regional Research Center, New Orleans
- West Baton Rouge Museum, Baton Rouge

MISSISSIPPI

- Civil War Interpretive Center, Corinth
- College Hill Presbyterian Church, Oxford
- French Camp Historical Area, French Camp
- Governor's Mansion, Jackson
- John C. Stennis Space Center, Bay St. Louis
- Manship House, Jackson
- Meridian Museum Of Art, Meredian
- New Capitol, Jackson
- Northeast Mississippi Museum, Corinth
- Rowan Oak, Oxford
- St. Peter's Cemetery, Oxford
- Tupelo National Battlefield, Tupelo
- University of Mississippi: Barnard Observatory, Oxford
- University of Mississippi: Center for the Study of Southern Culture, Oxford
- Winterville Mounds State Park, Greenville

NORTH CAROLINA

- Ackland Art Museum, Chapel Hill
- Botanical Gardens of Asheville, Asheville
- Brunswick Town State Historic Site, Wilmington
- Fort Raleigh National Historic Site, Nags Head
- Great Smoky Mountains National Park, Asheville
- Hickory Museum of Art, Hickory
- J. C. Raulsten Arboretum at N.C. State University, Raleigh
- Linville Falls, Asheville
- North Carolina Botanical Garden, Chapel Hill
- North Carolina Museums of Art, History, or Natural Sciences, Raleigh
- Reedy Creek Park and Nature Preserve, Charlotte
- Town Creek Indian Mound State Historic Site, Mt. Gilead
- Wake Forest Museum of Anthropology, Winston-Salem

SOUTH CAROLINA

- Carolina Sandhills National Wildlife Refuge, Long Creek
- Chattooga National Wild and Scenic River, Columbia
- Clemson University: Cooper Library, Lee Gallery, Clemson
- Congaree Swamp National Monument, Columbia
- Duke World of Energy, Seneca
- Hartsville Museum, Florence
- John Rutledge House, Charleston
- Magnolia Cemetery, Charleston
- Riverfront Park and Canal, Columbia
- Rose Hill Plantation State Historic Site, Union
- South Carolina Botanical Garden, Clemson
- State House, Columbia
- The Battery, Charleston

TENNESSEE

- Bicentennial Mall State Park, Nashville
- Downtown Presbyterian Church, Nashville
- East Tennessee Historical Center, Knoxville
- Edwin and Percy Warner Parks, Nashville
- Fort Donelson National Battlefield, Dover
- Jack Daniels Distillery, Lynchburg
- Lenoir Museum, Norris
- Mud Island River Park, Memphis
- Red Clay State Historic Park, Cleveland
- Stones River National Battlefield, Murfreesboro
- Tennessee National Wildlife Refuge, Paris
- Tennessee Walking Horse Museum, Lynchburg
- The Graphite Reactor, Oak Ridge

VIRGINIA

- Booker T. Washington National Monument, Roanoke
- Canal Walk, Richmond
- Christ Church, Alexandria
- Fredericksburg National Cemetery, Fredericksburg
- Hampton Roads Naval Museum, Norfolk
- Lyceum History Museum, Alexandria
- Maymont Park, Richmond
- Old Presbyterian Meeting House, Alexandria
- Radford University Art Museum, Roanoke
- Richmond National Battlefield Park, Richmond
- St. John's Episcopal Church, Richmond
- Torpedo Factory Art Center, Alexandria
- University of Virginia Art Museum, Charlottesville

WEST VIRGINIA

- Blackwater Falls State Park, Davis
- Bluestone National Scenic River, Beckley
- Camp Washington-Carver, Charleston
- Carnifex Ferr Battlefield State Park, Summersville
- Core Arboretum, Morgantown
- Huntington Museum of Art, Huntington
- Lost River State Park, Mathias
- National Radio Astronomy Observatory, Charleston
- Old Stone Church, Lewisburg
- Patterson House, Charleston
- State Capitol, Charleston
- West Virginia Cultural Center, Charleston
- West Virignia State Museum/Cultural Center, Charleston

It was THIS BIG

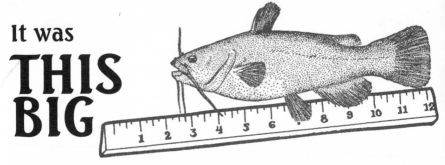

Humans have told stories since the beginning of time, when good communication literally could mean the difference between life and death. Telling stories is a way to share information, a link to our families and communities, a way to keep the past alive, or sometimes just the lead-up to a good joke.

Now, maybe it's not that serious anymore (unless you're fighting for bragging rights), but we doubt there is a person in the South who cannot tell a good story. It's genetic. So turn off the television, and tell (or listen to) a good story instead. There's nothing better.

There are actually storytelling festivals that hold **contests**, with prizes and everything. The National Storytelling Festival is just one; check your local listings for more. (Ooops…sorry! We mean, contact your local library for suggestions of local storytelling festivals).

Here's a real fish story for you: in the South, catfish can grow as large as a child. The record for a blue catfish, caught in Illinois, is 124 pounds! That's a big kid…

**National Storytelling Festival
Jonesborough, Tennessee
(800) 962-9392
www.storytellingcenter.com**

Considered one of the top 100 events in the country.
More than thirty years old, this 3-day festival is held annually in October in northeastern Tennessee and is the model for many other storytelling events.

The Official State...

BIRD

AL Yellowhammer (*Colaptes auratus linnaeus*)

AR Mockingbird (*Mimus polyglottis*)

GA Brown Thrasher (*Toxostoma rufum*)

KY Cardinal (*Cardinalis cardinalis*)

LA Brown Pelican (*Pelecanus occidentalis*)

MS Mockingbird (*Mimus polyglottos*)

NC Cardinal (*Cardinalis cardinalis*)

SC Carolina Wren (*Thryothorus ludovicianus*)

TN Mockingbird (*Mimus polyglottos*)

VA Cardinal (*Cardinalis cardinalis*)

WV Cardinal (*Cardinalis cardinalis*)

FLOWER

AL Camellia (*Camellia japonica*)

AR Apple blossom (*Pyrus coronaria*)

GA Cherokee Rose (*Rosa laevigata*)

KY Goldenrod (*Solidago altissima*)

LA Magnolia (*Magnolia grandiflora*)

MS Magnolia (*Magnolia grandiflora*)

NC Flowering Dogwood (*Cornus florida*)

SC Yellow Jessamine (*Gelsemium sempervirens*)

TN Iris (*Iridaceae*)

VA American Dogwood (*Cornus florida*)

WV Big Laurel (*Rhododendron maximum*)

TREE

AL Southern Longleaf Pine (*Pinus palustris miller*)

AR Loblolly Pine (*Pinus taeda*)

GA Live Oak (*Quercus virginiana*)

KY Yellow-poplar (*Liriodendron tulipifera*)

LA Baldcypress (*Taxodium distichum*)

MS Magnolia (*Magnolia grandiflora*)

NC Pine (*Pinus*)

SC Cabbage Palmetto (*Inodes palmetto*)

TN Tulip Poplar (*Liriodendron tulipifera*)

VA Dogwood (*Cornus florida*)

WV Sugar Maple (*Acer saccharum*)

WILD ANIMAL

AL Black Bear (*Ursus americanus pallas*)

AR White-tail deer (*Odocoileus virginianus*)

GA Right Whale (*Balaenidae*)

KY Gray Squirrel (*Sciurus carolinensis*)

LA Black Bear (*Ursus americanus*)

MS White-tail deer (*Odocoileus virginianus*) and Red Fox (*Vulpes vulpes*)

NC Gray Squirrel (*Sciurus carolinensis*)

SC White-tail Deer (*Odocoileus virginianus*)

TN Raccoon (*Procyon lotor*)

VA Virginia Big-Eared Bat (*Corynorhinus townsendii virginianus*)

WV Black Bear (*Ursus americanus*)

WILDFLOWER

AL Oak-leaf Hydrangea (*Hydrangea quercifolia*)

GA Azalea (*Rhododendron spp.*)

LA Louisiana Iris (*Iris giganticaerulea*)

MS Coreopsis (*Coreopsis gladiata*)

NC Carolina Lily (*Lilium michauxii*)

SC Goldenrod (*Solidago altissima*)

TN Passion Flower (*Passiflora incarnata*)

BUG MORSE CODE

Lightning bugs, or fireflies—the small blinking creatures that light up summer nights—are actually beetles of the family *Lampyridae*. Soon after the sun goes down, hundreds of flickering lights appear, dancing over the grass or rising up into the trees.

The male firefly emits distinctive flash patterns of light to attract a mate. The females signal in response from perches in or near the ground, and through a series of flashes they find each other and mate. Flash patterns range from continuous glows to single flashes or multi-pulsed flashes.

Each species of firefly sends different mating signals, and impregnated females of some species actually mimic the codes of other lightning bugs to lure a male down, where he is promptly captured and eaten!

The flashing fireflies are true wonders of nature, emitting a cold light known as bioluminescence, an ability they share with many marine organisms. The firefly combines the chemical lucerferin with oxygen and the enzyme luciferase to produce light in specially adapted cells in the tail section of the abdomen. Over 95% of the energy is converted into light, unlike a light bulb, which inefficiently converts only 10% of electrical energy into light, the rest being lost as heat.

Although other insects can produce light, fireflies are the only ones that can flash their light on and off in distinct signals. It's still a mystery whether they control the on-off switching of the light by nerve cells or oxygen supplied to the abdomen by abdominal trachea.

A lab in California, Promega Biosciences, actually *pays* for fireflies to be used for research. The bioluminescence of the lightning bugs is used in food safety testing as well as research on such diseases as Alzheimer's, cystic fibrosis, and some cancers. The going rate is about $1.45 for every 100 lightning bugs.

THE INVINCIBLE FIRE ANT

The fire ant, *Solenopsis invicta*—appropriately named as *invicta* means "invincible" in Latin—is a formidable species notorious for its aggressive nature and multiple stings. Accidentally introduced into the U.S. via Brazilian cargo entering the port of Mobile, Alabama in the 1930s, the fire ant has become a major pest.

When disturbed, fire ants bite to get a grip, then sting repeatedly from the abdomen, injecting a toxic alkaloid venom. The ring of stings develops into a swollen red area, accompanied by pain, itching, and burning. Small blisters form at the sting site within four hours and develop into pustules in 6 to 24 hours. (It's as painful and gross as it sounds.) Antihistamines are the usual treatment unless people are particularly sensitive to allergic reactions and should seek medical help. Clean wounds well, making sure not to break any blisters.

Fire ant colonies are symmetrical, dome-shaped mounds up to two feet high. Beneath the visible mound inter-connected galleries and chambers may extend three to four feet and have several exits. An average colony can contain 100,000 to 500,000 workers and several queens, and they will attack aggressively. Fire ants nest in the soil, often near moist areas, in rotten logs, build-

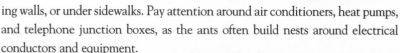

ing walls, or under sidewalks. Pay attention around air conditioners, heat pumps, and telephone junction boxes, as the ants often build nests around electrical conductors and equipment.

Are humans and ants really that different? Ants raise "livestock", develop complex societies, communicate with each other, are master builders, practice slavery, and wage war. Hmmm……

This is one import from Brazil we could have lived without but the Brazilian phorid fly, *Apocephalus*, has also been introduced into the southern United States for biological con-trol of the red fire ant. This ingenious fly hovers over ant mounds before darting down and injecting torpedo-like eggs in the head of a fire ant. The larvae decapitate the ant by eating the contents of its head and emerge several days later. Seems fair.

THE CHOMPING
CHIGGER

The microscopic chigger is a crafty little critter, attacking campers, picnickers, hikers, and fishermen, looking for its next protein meal. The six-legged chigger is actually the larvae of the harvest mite, those creatures that look like small, velvety red spiders you find in the garden when turning the soil in spring.

Crawling rapidly over the ground, chiggers climb onto feet and legs looking for a nice, snug place to settle in, usually where clothing fits tightly like ankles and waists, or where the flesh is tender and wrinkled, such as armpits, elbows, back of the knees, and groin.

Chiggers pierce the skin and inject a salivary secretion containing powerful digestive enzymes that break down ingested skin cells and cause surrounding tissue to harden, forming a straw-like feeding tube. Left to feed, the chigger larva is engorged within four days, and then drops from its host, leaving a severely itchy red welt with a hard, white center. Welts, swelling, itching or fever usually develop within three to six hours after exposure.

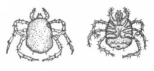

The chigger, top view (l) and botton view (r).

Chiggers thrive in areas of high humidity (but of course) and are very common throughout the South. They're most likely to be found where vegetation is thick and shady. Avoid sitting on the grass without a blanket unless you don't mind being part of the chigger buffet! You can test for areas of heavy infestation by placing a square of black paper vertically in the grass. If it becomes covered with tiny yellow or pink dots moving around, chiggers are present.

Washing well after possible exposure is the best method of control, and clothes need to be washed in hot water and dried in a high-heat dryer cycle to kill them. DEET is an excellent repellent for chiggers, and applying antihistamine creams or astringents such as a dilute bleach solution to affected areas helps reduce itching.

It Gets Worse Before It Gets Better

Some folk remedies to ease the intense itch of chigger bites include: Preparation H; Listerine; very hot water; nail polish (no specific color noted); meat tenderizer; alcohol (the other kind); calamine lotion; cold cream; and baby oil.

Where the Buffalo Roam

Herds of elk and bison used to graze the prairie grasses of Kentucky, until European settlers moving westward hunted without restraint, decimating the herds to extinction by the 1850s. By 1900 even white-tail deer were scarce. As pioneers settled the land and suppressed fires, vegetation changed. Forests took over and the wildlife changed with it.

In 1975, biologists discovered a small patch of native prairie grass in the Land Between the Lakes, and tested controlled burning. Soon other areas sprang up with the prairie grasses from seeds that had lain dormant for *centuries*, awaiting fire to germinate.

A 700-acre section has now been enclosed to reestablish the original prairie habitat. Opened in 1996, the Elk and Bison Prairie replicates the native habitat of elk and bison that once thrived in western Kentucky. Herds graze freely, living with deer, bobcats, coyotes, and wild turkeys. Red-tail hawks, owls, bald eagles, and an array of birdlife now inhabit the grasslands that have returned after an absence of 200 years.

The elk herd, populated from Canadian elk, numbers about 60. The bison herd (established some years earlier at LBL and moved to the prairie habitat in 1996) now has about 100 animals. Year-round wildlife viewing is encouraged in this wonderful preserve.

Visit *www.lbl.org* for more info.

Herds of elk have been reestablished in the Appalachian Mountains of eastern Kentucky. The elk population now stands at about 5,500, and elk hunting is allowed once again.

Bring the Smelling Salts—the Goat Has Fainted!

A most unusual breed of goats, known for its peculiar habit of "fainting" when startled, can trace its origins back to the 1880s in Marshall County, Tennessee.

The fainting goat is a domestic breed whose external muscles freeze for 10 to 15 seconds when the goat is frightened or startled, causing the animal to fall over, stiff-legged, in an apparent faint. Still fully conscious, the goat soon picks itself up and walks off, sometimes in an awkward shuffle. A spooked herd looks a bit like a slapstick comedy, as goats run and fall over, legs high in the air or stuck straight out. The characteristic is caused by a hereditary genetic disorder called myotonic congenita. Older goats are more adept at dealing with the problem, often leaning against a fence or barn to stay upright.

The goats' first recorded appearance goes back to a reclusive visitor named Tinsley, who arrived in Caney Spring one day bringing along four "bulgy eyed" goats and a "sacred cow". He stayed long enough to marry a local woman, then sold his goats to Dr. H.H. Mayberry and departed. He took the cow with him, but left his wife behind.

The doctor bred the three does and buck, and today's fainting goats have descended from that small herd. Primarily used for meat, the goats were often used to protect sheep from coyotes and dogs. The fainting goat would provide an easy meal for the predator while the sheep escaped.

The goats are a small breed, generally 17 to 25 inches tall, weighing anywhere from 50 to 165 pounds. They have large, prominent eyes, and exist in all colors and markings, with either long or short hair. The females commonly produce triplets, and due to their regular "isometric exercises" are in better shape, with 40% more meat, than similarly sized goats.

Facing extinction in the 1980s, the goats have seen a resurgence thanks to fainting goat enthusiasts. The city of Lewisburg, TN now honors their indigenous fainting critters with an annual goat festival, highlighted by the World Championship Fainting Goat Show. Try calling 1-866-96-GOATS for festival dates and more information.

What Was That?

Want to identify the birds at your backyard feeder? Here are some suggestions:

- Purchase a good field guide for your area.

- Obtain a checklist of the birds you're likely to see in your area; these can be obtained online or from local bird-watching groups.

- Learn to look for field marks, such as the bill (short/long, thick/thin), the tail (long/short, pointed up/down, forked/pointed/flat), eye ring, legs, wing bars, color, and more.

- Observe how the bird flies: does it flap rapidly then glide, go straight or in a zig-zag?

- How big is it? As big as a sparrow, a robin, a pigeon?

- Learn to identify birds' calls and songs.

- Take a photograph—it will help you remember.

Creating a Bird-Friendly Garden

It's simple! Birds need what we need: food, shelter, and water. Most important, don't use pesticides in your garden, as many birds are susceptible to even trace amounts.

Shelter

Plant trees and shrubs for nesting space, as well as cover from predators. These are also great places to hang feeders. Put up birdhouses too.

Food

Annuals that flower and go to seed (such as sunflowers), as well as flowering trees and sunflowers provide natural food, as do insects that inhabit the plants. Feed a variety of foods to attract different birds.

Water

Fresh water is essential for bathing and drinking; moving water is best (remember, a stagnant pool breeds mosquitos).

WHAT WAS THAT?

There are several Web sites that specialize in bird identification, but we like this one:
www.whatbird.com.
Enter field marks one at a time, then get a list of birds that meet the criteria.

THE LIVING FOSSIL

They may not be the most attractive animal in the woods, but learn to love your neighborhood opossum—it's a good neighbor. One of the few animals living today that has survived since the age of dinosaurs, the quiet, nocturnal 'possum makes use of what food it finds in its environment—it helps keep the environment clean as it consumes carrion, bugs, snails, slugs, even mice and rats. It eats overripe fruit before it rots, and feels free to help itself to pet food left out overnight too. So next time you see one of nature's sanitation engineers, make it welcome!

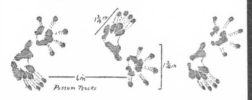

Possum Tracks

'POSSUM FACTS

- The opossum is the only marsupial in North America; it is not a rodent.
- A low blood temperature means rabies is almost unknown in 'possums.
- Opossum fur is very soft and was once commonly used in the bathtub as a wash "cloth."
- Their robust immune system is a partial or complete protection against disease and, often, snakebite.
- Opossums are nomadic; they go where food and water are easily accessible.
- The hairless, prehensile tail is not strong enough to support the weight of an adult 'possum.
- Babies are carried in the pouch and later on the mother's back. Infants are so small at birth that 20 could fit into a teaspoon.
- The opossum has 50 teeth, more than any North American land mammal.

PLAYING 'POSSUM

The curled-up, seemingly dead opossum is not "acting"—this defense mechanism, in which a threatened or injured 'possum plays dead, is an involuntary physiological response. With teeth bared, saliva drools from the mouth, and a foul-smelling fluid is expelled from the anal glands—mimicking the appearance of death. It can be poked and prodded, but nothing happens, and often the predator moves on. Don't assume a catatonic 'possum is dead; if you want to help, remove it from immediate danger and leave it in a quiet place from which it can escape. When it regains consciousness, it will escape on its own!

COUNTRY MUSIC LEGEND GEORGE JONES'S NICKNAME IS THE POSSUM.

Return of the
IVORY-BILLED WOODPECKER?

The spectacular ivory-billed woodpecker, thought to be extinct in the United States for the past 60 years, may have been rediscovered in Arkansas in February, 2004.

A chance sighting in the Cache River National Wildlife Refuge sparked a year-long joint search by The Nature Conservancy and Cornell Laboratory of Ornithology, confirming evidence that the ivory-billed woodpecker may indeed be present. The team reported multiple fleeting views of a bird thought to be the ivory-bill, video footage, and recordings of its distinctive double knock.

Among the world's largest woodpeckers, the ivory-billed woodpecker *Campephilus principalis* once ranged through swampy forests in the southeastern and lower Mississippi Valley states, from Florida and North Carolina to Arkansas and eastern Texas. The ivory-bill averages 20 inches in length, and has a white patch on its wing feathers, which form a "saddle" when the bird is perched. The males have a prominent scarlet crest, and the females sport a black crest. The unique double knock ("BAM-bam") of an ivory-bill pounding on a tree is believed to indicate its presence and mark its territory.

John James Audubon described the ivory-billed woodpecker as an aristocrat in appearance: its great stature, heavy, ivory-colored, chisel-tipped bill, pale lemon-yellow eyes, crisp black-and-white markings, distinctive crest, and long, lean appearance.

The woodpecker feeds on insects, primarily beetle larvae, and fruits and nuts, stripping bark from dead trees in its search for food. Ornithologists speculate the ivory-bill has a lifespan of 20 to 30 years. They are believed to mate for life, and a pair needs at least a six-square-mile habitat of mature hardwood forest.

To ensure the protection of their habitat since the recent search, The Nature Conservancy has acquired more than 18,000 acres of the Big Woods near the Cache River and White River national wildlife refuges in Arkansas. The research continues; let's hope for the best.

WATCH OUT FOR PEPE LE PEW!

Skunks are common across the U.S. and very prevalent throughout the South. They only spray when threatened, and exhibit certain warning signs before spraying. If you see one bushing out its fur, shaking its tail, stamping the ground, growling, or turning its head and spitting...*run*! A skunk can fire a 15-foot fan-patterned spray with precision accuracy, and can store enough potent oil in two walnut-sized glands for about five to six sprays.

Nosy dogs are the most common recipients of a skunk's foul-smelling spray. If your dog gets "skunked", one remedy is to flush the face and mouth with fresh, running water, bathe the dog, and then pour on the following mixture:

- 1 quart hydrogen peroxide
- ¼ cup baking soda
- 1 teaspoon liquid detergent

After five or ten minutes, rinse the liquid off with water and repeat if necessary. Be careful not to store this mixture in a closed container, as it will explode. (Yet another problem.) The main hazards skunks pose is spraying, although they are carriers of rabies.

Hands Off!

That cute, bandit-faced raccoon could kill you: raccoons are the primary carriers of rabies in the South. Skunks, foxes, and bats are also common carriers, but the raccoon is the worst offender. Even a seemingly healthy wild animal can incubate the virus for *up to twelve weeks*, and may show no signs of illness during incubation. The disease is spread by bite wounds or contact with the infected animal's saliva; without prompt treatment, it is always fatal. Although rabies affects livestock as well as domestic pets, unvaccinated cats and dogs are the most likely means of transmission to humans. If they bite a person, they can legally be required to undergo quarantine or testing by a state lab, which could mean decapitation to analyze the brain. The viral encephalitis affects an animal's nervous system, eventually manifesting symptoms including unusual behavior, partial paralysis, inability to swallow (foaming at the mouth), agitation, and aggression. Unusual behavior in wild animals means they may appear lethargic and tame—they are not. Never handle wild animals; if you find one that appears sick, contact a qualified wildlife rescuer.

RABIES SYMPTOMS

Unusual behavior

Partial paralysis

Inability to swallow
(foaming at the mouth)

Agitation

Aggression

Rabies is found in all U.S. States except Hawaii.

BEWARE THE SNAKE IN THE GRASS...

Most snakes are harmless, feeding on insects, rats, mice, and other rodents. The venomous ones typically hunt at night, spending their days holed up in piles of brush, stacked firewood, rock crevices, and around streambeds. You're most likely to encounter a snake when hiking through tall grass, or clearing away brush and lumber outside. Leaving a snake to slither away on its own, or giving a gentle prod from a long stick, is much better than confronting it. Most snakes will not strike unless startled or cornered.

In the South there are four types of venomous snakes to worry about: the coral snake, and three pit vipers—the copperhead, the water moccasin (also called the cottonmouth), and the rattlesnake.

Coral snakes' poison is a neurotoxin, shutting down the nervous system and resulting in cardiac arrest and respiratory failure. This candy-colored banded snake matures at 20 to 30 inches, sporting red, yellow and black body rings. It has an unpredictable temperament and strikes quickly. The coral snake is very secretive, preferring dry woods and scrubby areas.

Coral snake

Copperhead snake

Copperheads and water moccasins are in the moccasin family. Copperheads can grow to 50 inches and have rusty-colored heads and pink and brown body markings. They live in shady areas with heavy ground cover, where they are well-camouflaged; because of this, they can be easily stepped on, stimulating a reactive strike. Their venom is less toxic than rattlesnakes and coral snakes, and they are generally non-aggressive, giving *you* time to move out of *their* way.

Water moccasins are dark-colored water snakes, with a head wider than the neck. They may be dark gray or black, or have dark cross-bands with serrated edges. The white "cotton" mouth is visible when they defensively open their jaws. They are found in swamps, rivers, rice fields and waterways. When disturbed, they may drop into the water and swim away with their head held high. They should be given a wide berth.

Rattlesnakes can strike from any position with a range equal to half its body length—sometimes difficult to gauge from a coiled snake! They don't always rattle first, and can strike with blinding speed, so don't assume you'll get any warning. Found in all kinds of habitat, if you do hear their warning rattle, freeze! Find out where the snake is and retreat slowly. The Eastern diamondback rattlesnake is considered the most dangerous snake in the eastern U.S. Responsible for 66% of all venomous snake bites in the country, the rattlesnake's long fangs inject a large amount of venom, often causing instant numbing, with rapid swelling and pain.

Rattlesnake

The best advice when you're hiking or working outdoors is to wear protective clothing, make plenty of noise, and stay alert.

Snakebite First Aid

Various first aid measures are controversial, but widely accepted first aid includes:

- Clean and disinfect the wound
- Keep the victim still, or as little exertion as possible
- Remove jewelry and tight fitting clothes
- Mark the border or the advancing swelling every 15 minutes with a pen
- Maintain the bitten limb at heart level, or slightly lower

If tissue destruction is likely to occur, the use of tourniquets is not always advised. Seek medical attention immediately.

Hemorrhagic and neurotoxic elements in snake venom destroy red blood cells and cause the victim to bleed to death, or shut down the central nervous system, resulting in cardiac and respiratory failure.

OUR WILDLIFE HERITAGE— THREATENED

Endangered Species in the South

Bat, gray (*Myotis grisescens*)
Bat, Indiana (*Myotis sodalis*)
Bat, Virginia big-eared (*Corynorhinus townsendii virginianus*)
Bear, American black (*Ursus americanus*)
Bear, Louisiana black (*Ursus americanus luteolus*)
Crane, Mississippi sandhill (*Grus canadensis pulla*)
Crane, whooping (*Grus Americana*)
Curlew, Eskimo (*Numenius borealis*)
Eagle, bald (*Haliaeetus leucocephalus*)
Falcon, peregrine (*Falco peregrinus*)
Manatee, West Indian (*Trichechus manatus*)
Mouse, Alabama beach (*Peromyscus polionotus ammobates*)
Panther, Florida (*Felis concolor coryi*)
Pelican, brown (*Pelecanus occidentalis*)
Plover, piping (*Charadrius melodus*)
Plover, southeastern snowy (*Charadrius alexandrinus tenuirostris*)
Prairie chicken, Attwater's greater (*Tympanuchus cupido attwateri*)
Puma, eastern (*Puma concolor couguar*)
Sea turtle, green (*Chelonia mydas*)
Sea turtle, hawksbill (*Eretmochelys imbricata*)
Sea turtle, Kemp's Ridley (*Lepidochelys kempii*)
Sea turtle, leatherback (*Dermochelys coriacea*)
Sea turtle, loggerhead (*Caretta caretta*)
Shrew, Dismal Swamp southeastern (*Sorex longirostris fisheri*)
Snake, black pine (*Pituophis melanoleucus lodingi*)
Snake, eastern indigo (*Drymarchon corais couperi*)

Whooping Crane

Green Sea Turtle

The Endangered Species Act of 1973 created a list of flora and fauna, classifying them as endangered, threatened, or candidates for later listing. This is the list for the South. (Some species may not be endangered in all states, but we are listing all in alpha order for simplicity.)

Snake, hognosed (*Heterodon simus*)
Stork, wood (*Mycteria americana*)
Squirrel, Carolina northern flying (*Glaucomys sabrinus coloratus*)
Squirrel, Delmarva Peninsula fox (*Sciurus niger cinereus*)
Squirrel, Virginia northern flying (*Glaucomys sabrinus fuscus*)
Tern, interior least (*Sterna antillarum athalassos*)
Tern, roseate (*Sterna dougallii dougallii*)
Tortoise, gopher (*Gopherus polyphemus*)
Turtle, Alabama red-bellied (*Pseudemys alabamensis*)
Turtle, bog (*Clemmys muhlenbergii*)
Turtle, flattened musk (*Sternotherus depressus*)
Turtle, ringed map (*Graptemys oculifera*)
Turtle, yellow-blotched map (*Graptemys flavimaculata*)

Roseate Tern

Warbler, Bachman's (*Vermivora bachmanii*)
Warbler, Kirtland's (*Dendroica kirtlandii*)
Whale, blue (*Balaenoptera musculus*)
Whale, finback (*Balaenoptera physalus*)
Whale, humpback (*Megaptera novaeangliae*)
Whale, right (*Balaena glacialis*)
Whale, Sei (*Balaenoptera borealis*)
Whale, sperm (*Physeter macrocephalus*)
Wolf, red (*Canis rufus*)
Woodpecker, ivory-billed (*Campephilus principalis*)
Woodpecker, red-cockaded (*Picoides borealis*)
Wren, Berwick's (*Thryomanes berwickii*)

* = threatened

Humpback Whale

Success by Inches

The bald eagle, American alligator, and peregrine falcon are great success stories in American conservation efforts, but efforts to recover these animals started well before the Environmental Species Act went into effect. For example, the Bald Eagle Act of 1940 made it illegal to hunt it, and the 1972 ban on DDT put 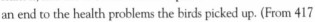 an end to the health problems the birds picked up. (From 417 breeding pairs in 1963, there are 9,250 pairs in 2006.) Although it is currently on the threatened list, plans are underway to remove the bald eagle entirely.

Bald Eagle

But placing a species on the list draws attention to its peril, and very often gets the public involved. Such was the case with the peregrine falcon, whose population has increased significantly as hundreds of people participated in the raising of thousands of falcons in captivity for their eventual reintroduction to the wild.

Other success stories include:

- Brown pelican is fully recovered and has been removed from the list in all but Louisiana and Mississippi
- Gray bats have experienced a population increase as measures such as cave gates and informational signs have improved breeding success
- Red wolves have been successfully reintroduced into the wild in North Carolina
- Red-cockaded woodpeckers have experienced a population increase due to habitat protection measures undertaken by the Georgia-Pacific Railroad; the birds also responded well to artificial cavity and translocation programs
- Delmarva Peninsula fox squirrel population has stabilized
- Northern flying squirrel numbers have increased since the species' listing in 1985, when there were just 10 individuals (now there are 69 known)
- Whooping cranes have increased from 54 birds in 1967 to 436 in 2003.

"Most wild animals get into the world and out of it without being noticed. Nevertheless we at last sadly learn that they are all subject to the vicissitudes of fortune like ourselves."

—JOHN MUIR
(1838–1914)

Success is sometimes measured in inches, but it is measured.

DID YOU KNOW?

- A fox's footprints are similar to a dog's, but the fox places one foot directly in front of the other, in a straight line.
- North Carolina has more species of newts than the rest of the world combined.
- A bird feeding on blackberries excretes the seeds less than 15 minutes later (usually on your car).
- Opossums have one of the shortest gestation periods, bearing the young 12 to 13 *days* after conception. (That's why there are still swarms of them even though so many are hit by cars.)
- Catfish have 100,000 taste buds (and yet, they are bottom feeders....)
- Armadillos always bear four babies of the same sex. The fertilized eggs split in four, resulting in four identical armadillos. (And 'dillos can walk under water. We're doomed.)
- Wild turkeys can fly for short distances up to 55 mph and run at speeds up to 25 mph.
- Bees collect nectar from 2,000 flowers to make one tablespoon of honey.
- The blood of mammals is red, the blood of insects is yellow, and the blood of lobsters is blue. (Q: What color is a lawyer's blood? A: Trick question.)
- Mockingbirds can imitate any sound, from a squeaking door to a cat's meow.
- Chickens that lay brown eggs have red ear lobes. There is a genetic link.
- Peregrine falcons can reach 198 mph in a dive.
- Mississippi produces more than 70% of the world's supply of farm-raised catfish.
- Moles are able to tunnel through 300 feet of earth a day. (But of course.)
- Ruby-throated hummingbirds fly as many as 600 miles non-stop across the Gulf of Mexico on their winter migration to Mexico.
- Certain frogs can be frozen solid, then thawed and continue living.
- Crickets hear through their knees.
- Most of the oysters eaten in the United States come from Louisiana.
- An electric eel can produce a shock of up to 650 volts.
- The average garden variety caterpillar has 248 muscles in its head.

WELL, Forgive Us for Bragging!

Several of the top ten spots of the hottest cities in the nation to expand to, or to relocate to, are located in the South. If you're looking to start a business or to expand, consider these cities:

#1 Nashville, TN

#3 Atlanta, GA

#6 Charlotte, NC

#7 Memphis, TN

#9 Knoxville, TN

#10 Birmingham, AL

Source: As listed by *Expansion Management* magazine ("America's 50 Hottest Cities", 2006)

Can You Imagine the Round-up!

One of the more unusual business ideas that we've heard about is raising fresh-water prawns. As tobacco fields are turning fallow, some farmers have turned to aquaculture for help. Prawns pretty much just eat prawn-chow, and mature in about 120 days, which means some locations in long-season climates could raise two herds. Roping them does require an awfully small lasso, and you have to be really careful you don't crush them.

WHEN IT
ABSOLUTELY,
POSITIVELY
HAS TO BE THERE OVERNIGHT

As founder of one of the world's most successful overnight courier services that has grown into a $20 billion global transportation and logistics company, the name of Frederick W. Smith is synonymous with FedEx.

A Yale graduate and former U.S. Marine, Fred Smith officially launched Federal Express operations from his Memphis, Tennessee base on April 17, 1973, with a fleet of 14 small aircraft. On that first night, the company delivered 186 packages to 25 U.S. cities from Rochester, New York, to Miami, Florida.

Developing an efficient distribution system for overnight air freight through its Memphis hub, Smith revolutionized global business practices and now serves 211 countries using more than 640 aircraft and 95,000 ground vehicles. The company's 215,000 employees and independent contractors worldwide handle an average of five million shipments every day. FedEx operations have made Memphis International Airport one of the largest air cargo airports in the world.

The company's business expanded dramatically when it acquired the Flying Tigers in 1989. Today FedEx Express has the world's largest all-cargo air fleet, which in a 24-hour period travels nearly 500,000 miles. Added to its ground couriers' log of 2.5 million miles a day, the distance covered is equivalent to 100 trips around the earth.

Fred Smith was inducted into the Tennessee Aviation Hall of Fame in 2002 to honor his achievements as founder of Federal Express.

FEDEX FACTS:

FedEx planes are named after the children of employees.

The United States Postal Service is one of FedEx's biggest customers, contracting them to fly over one billion dollars worth of packages per year for delivery.

In 2003, FedEx delivered two giant pandas from Beijing, China to the Memphis Zoo.

SOUTHERN BUSINESS SUCCESS STORIES

Looking for investment ideas? Check out these Southern-based companies that may fit well with your portfolio ...

AFLAC INCORPORATED (NYSE: AFL)

www.aflac.com
Sells supplemental health/life insurance policies; one of largest in U.S.

BANK OF AMERICA CORPORATION (NYSE: BAC)

www.bankofamerica.com
First coast-to-coast bank, with more than 5,800 locations in 30 states; second-largest bank in the U.S. by assets.

BELLSOUTH CORPORATION (NYSE: BLS)

www.bellsouth.com
Third largest local phone company owns 40 percent of Cingular Wireless, the #1 mobile phone operator in the U.S.

CAREMARK RX, INC. (NYSE: CMX)

www.caremark.com
Prescription benefits management firm with a national network of more than 60,000 pharmacies.

CARMAX, INC. (NYSE: KMX)

www.carmax.com
The country's largest specialty used-car retailer with 70 retail units in more than 15 states.

CIRCUIT CITY STORES, INC. (NYSE: CC)

www.circuitcity.com
The #3 consumer electronics retailer in the U.S., with more than 630 stores in 45 states.

THE COCA-COLA COMPANY (NYSE: KO)

www.cocacola.com
Owns four of the top five soft-drink brands (Coca-Cola, Diet Coke, Fanta, and Sprite).

COCA-COLA BOTTLING CO. CONSOLIDATED (NASDAQ: COKE)

www.cokebottling.com
The #2 Coke bottler in the U.S.

DELTA AND PINE LAND COMPANY (NYSE: DLP)
www.deltaandpine.com
The nation's largest cottonseed breeder and producer.

DUKE ENERGY CORPORATION (NYSE: DUK)
www.duke-energy.com
Has 3.7 million electric customers and 1.7 million gas customers.

EARTHLINK, INC. (NASDAQ: ELNK)
www.earthlink.net
One of the largest ISPs in the U.S.

FEDEX CORPORATION (NYSE: FDX)
www.fedex.com
World's largest express transportation company.

FIRST HORIZON NATIONAL CORPORATION (NYSE: FHN)
www.fhnc.com
Banks and banking services.

GOODRICH CORPORATION (NYSE: GR)
www.goodrich.com
National leader in aerospace systems.

HCA INC. (NYSE: HCA)
www.hcahealthcare.com
Owns or operates 190 acute care, psychiatric, and rehabilitation hospitals in more than 20 states.

THE HOME DEPOT, INC. (NYSE: HD)
www.homedepot.com
World's largest home improvement chain and second-largest retailer in the U.S. with more than 2,000 stores in 50 states.

NATIONAL HEALTHCARE CORPORATION (AMEX: NHC)
www.nhccare.com
Operates more than 70 long-term health care centers in 12 states.

SRA INTERNATIONAL, INC. (NYSE: SRX)
www.sra.com
Information technology services.

SYNOVUS FINANCIAL CORP. (NYSE: SNV)
www.synovus.com
Holding company for small-town banks; more than 350 locations in Southeast.

WAL-MART (NYSE: WMT)
www.walmart.com
The largest retail company in the world based on sales. There have been eleven two-for-one stock splits.

TOP 20 RICHEST SOUTHERNERS

NAME	NET WORTH (BILLIONS.—YES, I SAID BILLIONS!)	RESIDENCE	SOURCE
1. Jim C. Walton	15.7	Bentonville, AR	Retailing/Wal-Mart
2. S. Robson Walton	15.6	Bentonville, AR	Retailing/Wal-Mart
3. Helen R. Walton	15.4	Bentonville, AR	Retailing/Wal-Mart
4. Anne Cox Chambers	12.5	Atlanta, GA	Media/Entertainment
5. Forrest Edward Mars Jr.	10	McLean, VA	Food/Candy
6. John Franklyn Mars	10	Arlington, VA	Food/Candy
7. James Goodnight	4.1	Cary, NC	Technology/SAS Institute
8. Martha R. Ingram & family	2.6	Nashville, TN	Service/Ingram Industries
9. Bernard Marcus	2.2	Atlanta, GA	Retailing/Home Depot
10. Clemmie Dixon Spangler Jr.	2.2	Charlotte, NC	Investments/Investments
11. John Sall	2.0	Cary, NC	Technology/SAS Institute
12. Thomas F. Frist Jr. & family	1.7	Nashville, TN	Healthcare/HCA Healthcare
13. Frederick Wallace Smith	1.7	Memphis, TN	Service/FedEx
14. Marguerite Harbert	1.5	Birmingham, AL	Service/Inheritance
15. Winnie Johnson-Marquart	1.5	Virginia Beach, VA	Manufacturing/SC Johnson&Sons
16. Ollen Bruton Smith	1.5	Charlotte, NC	Svc/Speedway Motorsports
17. Frank Batten Sr.	1.4	Virginia Beach, VA	Media Entertainment/ Landmark Communications
18. Arthur M. Blank	1.3	Atlanta, GA	Retailing/Home Depot
19. Brad M. Kelley	1.3	Nashville, TN	Agriculture/Tobacco
20. Phyllis Miller Taylor	1.2	New Orleans, LA	Oil & Gas / Taylor Energy

Source: Forbes.com "The 400 Richest Americans," 2005.

THE SOUTH'S 20 LARGEST PRIVATELY OWNED COMPANIES

1. Mars, Inc.	VA	Food Processing
2. Cox Enterprises	GA	Broadcasting
3. Unisource Worldwide	GA	Forest Products
4. MBM	NC	Food Distributing
5. Colonial Group	GA	Oil
6. Milliken & Co.	SC	Apparel & Textiles
7. HT Hackney	TN	Food Distributing
8. RaceTrac Petroleum	GA	Convenience Stores
9. Booz Allen Hamilton	VA	Business Services
10. InterTech Group	SC	Chemicals
11. Springs Industries	SC	Apparel & Textiles
12. Ergon	MS	Oil
13. Alex Lee	NC	Food Distributing
14. Belk	NC	Retail/General
15. Ingram Industries	TN	Multicompany
16. Vanguard Health Systems	TN	Healthcare/Services
17. Southwire	GA	Metal Fabricating
18. Houchens Industries	KY	Supermarkets
19. Quintiles Transnational	NC	Healthcare/Drugs
20. General Parts	NC	Auto Parts

Source: Forbes.com "The Largest Private Companies," 2005.

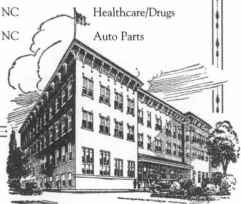

THE MOUTH OF THE SOUTH

Ted Turner is one of the world's richest, most successful businessmen—and one of the most outspoken. His habit of making controversial statements earned him his nickname, "Mouth of the South".

WHAT TED SAID

- You can never quit. Winners never quit, and quitters never win.

- I am anti-war, anti-poverty, anti-AIDS, anti-hunger, anti-hate, and I am pro-UN, pro-freedom, pro-competition, pro-democracy, pro-woman and pro-choice.

- War has been good to me from a financial standpoint but I don't want to make money that way. I don't want blood money.

- There's nothing wrong with being fired.

- The United States has got some of the dumbest people in the world. I want you to know that we know that.

- The media is too concentrated, too few people own too much. There's really five companies that control 90 percent of what we read, see and hear. It's not healthy.

- If you ever get a chance to buy a baseball team, do so. It's very fun.

- Sports is like a war without the killing.

- If I only had a little humility, I'd be perfect.

- As I started getting rich, I started thinking, "what the hell am I going to do with all this money?" … You have to learn to give.

- I've never run into a guy who could win at the top level in anything today and didn't have the right attitude, didn't give it everything he had, at least while he was doing it; wasn't prepared and didn't have the whole program worked out.

- All my life people have said that I wasn't going to make it.

- I know what I'm having 'em put on my tombstone: "I have nothing more to say."

I HAVE NOTHING MORE TO SAY...

Oprah Takes the Lead

Born January 29, 1954 in Kosciusko, Mississippi, to unmarried teenaged parents, Oprah Winfrey's current position as one of the wealthiest people in the world is a vast contrast to her childhood of poverty. Moving to Nashville, TN at age 14, Winfrey was still in high school when she began her broadcasting career at a local radio station, and by age 19 she'd become the youngest—and first African-American woman—to anchor the news at Nashville's WTVF-TV. Her talent for the business quickly manifested itself, and she became anchor at a larger, Baltimore station, and then a talk-show host there, before moving to Chicago in 1984. Talk is Oprah's forte—not to mention her empathy, curiosity, and humor—and she transformed a low-rated morning show to national syndication in just two years. In addition to her success on daytime television, Winfrey is an Academy Award–nominated actress, multiple Emmy-winner, producer, book critic, magazine publisher, and philanthropist.

Oprah's Angel Network, a public charity started in 1997, has raised more than $50 million dollars to date.

Oprah's production company—Harpo— is her name, spelled backwards.

The spelling of Oprah's name originally was to be "Orpah" from the Book of Ruth. A spelling error on her birth certificate changed it.

According to Forbes magazine, Oprah's net worth in 2006 was $1.4 billion.

Resources for Women in Business

U.S. SMALL BUSINESS ADMINISTRATION
Office of Women's Business
Ownership: Online Women's
Business Center
www.onlinewbc.gov/

WOMEN'S BUSINESS ENTERPRISE
NATIONAL COUNCIL
www.wbenc.org/

NATIONAL WOMEN'S BUSINESS COUNCIL
www.nwbc.gov/

BUSINESS WOMEN'S NETWORK
www.bwni.com

CATALYST
www.catalystwomen.org/

GREAT SOUTHERN EMPLOYERS*

Statistics say that many people change jobs every four years. So check out these corporations located in the South—they made Fortune's annual "100 Best Companies to Work For" list in 2006!

* If your name is not on page 82, read this…

AFLAC, COLUMBUS GA
What: A provider of health insurance policies.
Why: The largest on-site child-care facilities in Georgia, for starters; competitive salaries, a strong philanthropic policy, and just ask about Employee Appreciation Week!

ALSTON & BIRD, ATLANTA GA
What : A national, full-service law firm in business since 1893.
Why : A first-rate IT system keeps communication moving at the speed of light via a daily online newsletter. There's also monthly staff meetings and smaller meetings to keep everyone in the loop.

BOOZ ALLEN HAMILTON, McLEAN VA
What : A global strategy and technology consulting firm.
Why: A professional excellence awards program, an in-house university, and a partnership with Johns Hopkins to help employees earn MBAs.

CARMAX, GLEN ALLEN VA
What : The nation's largest no-haggle car retailer.
Why : Employees can buy any car left on the lot longer than 14 days for $200 over cost; employee time given to a nonprofit earns that organization an additional $10 per volunteer hour from CarMax.

CHILDREN'S HEATHCARE OF ATLANTA, ATLANTA GA
What : Pediatric hospitals.
Why : On-site child care, wellness program, baby showers, and concierge service to help employees with meal and trip reservations.

FEDEX, MEMPHIS TN
What : Courier service.
Why : The career path points up—policy is to promote from within, which keeps turnover to a miniscule 7 percent.

FIRST HORIZON NATIONAL, MEMPHIS TN
What : Banking, mortgages, financial services.
Why : A strong corporate culture that puts employee welfare first, with an expanding package of benefits.

HOMEBANC MORTGAGE, ATLANTA GA
What : Mortgage banking.
Why : Faith-based corporate culture puts employee satisfaction above customer satisfaction.

KIMLEY-HORN & ASSOCIATES, CARY NC
What : Engineering/architectural/environmental consulting services.
Why : Company pays entire health insurance premium (for employees and dependents), and is generous with bonuses and 401(k) plans.

MEMORIAL HEALTH, SAVANNAH GA
What : Hospital.
Why : Excellent benefits—tuition reimbursement, cheap onsite child care, adoption aid, and a hefty contribution to 401(k)—keep turnover low.

MILLIKEN & CO., SPARTANBURG SC
What : Textile and chemical manufacturer.
Why : Financially sound family-owned company hires the best and inspires fierce loyalty in employees.

SAS INSTITUTE, CARY NC
What : Business intelligence software and services.
Why : Unbelievable benefits—health-insurance premiums paid, three weeks of vacation after one year, unlimited sick leave, low-cost child care, and on-site medical facility.

SRA INTERNATIONAL, FAIRFAX VA
What : Technology and strategic consulting services to national security, government, and health care industries.
Why : In-house health and fitness program encourages employees (and dependents) to improve health.

SYNOVUS, COLUMBUS GA
What : Financial services holding company.
Why : Constant communication with employees—including monthly surveys—encourages honest feedback.

THE LIST

RANK	COMPANY	CITY	# U.S. EMPLOYEES
14.	HomeBanc Mortgage	Atlanta GA	1,342
19.	Alston & Bird	Atlanta GA	1,509
20.	Kimley-Horn & Associates	Cary NC	1,777
30.	SAS Institute	Cary NC	5,118
38.	Milliken & Co.	Spartanburg SC	9,300
45.	SRA International	Fairfax VA	3,986
47.	AFLAC	Columbus GA	4,034
57.	Synovus	Columbus GA	11,860
62.	Memorial Health	Savannah GA	4,301
64.	FedEx	Memphis TN	212,241
72.	Booz Allen Hamilton	McLean VA	15,582
76.	Children's Heathcare of Atlanta	Atlanta GA	4,910
85.	First Horizon National	Memphis TN	13,228
93.	CarMax	Glen Allen VA	11,400

Source: *Fortune.com*

SAM★WALTON
THE KING OF RETAIL

Sam Walton was a leader, not a follower, and blazed a path to become the world's discount chain king. At the time of his death in 1992, he ranked as the world's second richest man (behind Bill Gates), and Wal-Mart had grown into the world's largest company.

Born in 1918 near Kingfisher, Oklahoma, Sam Walton grew up during The Depression, learning the principles of hard work and thrift. His family lived in various towns throughout Missouri, and Walton thrived on new challenges, working many part-time jobs to help supplement his family's income. Always ambitious, he was the youngest boy in the state's history to become an Eagle Scout. He was both studious and athletic, and voted president of his school's student body in his senior year.

After graduating from the University of Missouri in 1940, Walton did a stint in the military, then launched into his retail career, buying a Ben Franklin five-and-dime franchise in Arkansas. His expertise grew as he pioneered many concepts that would proved enormously successful: Walton made sure store shelves remained stocked with a wide range of products; his stores stayed open later than the competition; and he pioneered the concept of discount merchandising. He also prowled the competition looking for good employees, and sweetened the deal by offering a share of the profits. The first Wal-Mart store opened in 1962 and became the world's number one retailer, as Walton soon

The exterior of a typical Wal-Mart store.
(Photo: Jared C. Benedict)

opened up a chain of discount stores across rural America. The early strategy of never moving into a town of more than 10,000 people meant Wal-Mart kept a small-town focus in the distribution and communication systems.

Walton's management style was popular with his employees, as he encouraged teamwork and offered profit sharing, stock options, and store discounts. The company valued its hometown identity, with its reputation for distinctive store greeters, providing college scholarships, and involvement in local charities. Walton took his 32-chain store public in 1970 and by 2003 the company had become the largest in the world, citing $256 billion in sales, $9.1 billion in profits and more than 4,900 stores around the world, including the popular Sam's Club.

Sam Walton was awarded the Presidential Medal of Freedom by President George H.W. Bush in 1992, and included in *Time* magazine's 1998 list of the "100 Most Influential People of the Twentieth Century." Walton died in on April 6, 1992, a man of vision and drive who revolutionized the retail world.

WAL-MART QUICK FACTS

Worldwide, Wal-Mart numbers about 1.8 million employees, including 1.3 million in the United States. (This makes Wal-Mart the nation's largest private employer.)

Wal-Mart has more than 6,500 stores in 15 countries.

About 176 million customers (worldwide) shop Wal-Mart weekly.

We're #2!!

Who's in the second spot for largest retail store? It's The Home Depot, founded in 1987 and based in Atlanta, GA. But it's the world's largest home-improvement store. For fiscal year 2005, The Home Depot had nearly $82 billion in sales. Not bad!

A NATIONAL CATASTROPHE

Hurricane Katrina lasted a long time, as hurricanes go. At its peak a Category 5, Katrina made landfall three times and devastated the Gulf Coast from Biloxi to New Orleans, virtually destroying the latter. Here's how the costliest and one of the deadliest hurricanes in U.S. history left its mark.

KATRINA BY THE NUMBERS

- Produced an estimated $75 billion in damages
- Sixth strongest Atlantic hurricane ever recorded
- Third strongest U.S. hurricane to make landfall ever recorded
- Eleventh named storm of the 2005 hurricane season
- Deaths caused: 1,836 (and counting)
- Highest recorded winds: 175 mph
- Highest recorded rainfall: 15 inches
- Twenty percent of marshland permanently overrun by water
- Sixteen National Wildlife Refuges closed

"If you can imagine, people coming onto the plane without shoes, maybe a garbage bag with all their worldly possessions— words cannot describe it."
—FRANK PHILLIPS,
Air Canada chief flight attendant, member of crew transporting survivors out and flying supplies in

KATRINA
A NEW ORLEANS TIMELINE

All times are Eastern Daylight Time unless otherwise noted.

TUESDAY, AUGUST 23, 2005
- 5:00 pm: the National Hurricane Center announces the formation of Tropical Depression Twelve over the Bahamas.

WEDNESDAY, AUGUST 24, 2005
- 11:00 am: Tropical Storm Twelve is upgraded to Tropical Storm Katrina. Katrina is born.

THURSDAY, AUGUST 25, 2005
- 7:00 am: FEMA National Response Coordination Center (NRCC) Red Team is activated.
- 5:00 pm: the National Hurricane Center upgrades the tropical storm to Hurricane Katrina.
- 7:00 pm: Hurricane Katrina makes landfall in Florida, Category 1, killing 6 people before exiting the state over the Everglades.

FRIDAY, AUGUST 26, 2005
- 11:30 am: Katrina is upgraded to Category 2.
- 5:00 pm: the National Hurricane Center issues an advisory, predicting that Katrina will soon be a Category 3 hurricane.
- 5:00 pm CDT: Louisiana Gov. Kathleen Babineaux Blanco declares a state of emergency for Louisiana. Mississippi Gov. Haley Barbour declares a state of emergency for Mississippi. Federal troops are deployed to Louisiana.
- 11:00 pm: the National Hurricane Center forecasts that Katrina will make landfall at Buras/Triumph, Louisiana, east of New Orleans.

SATURDAY, AUGUST 27, 2005
- 5:00 am: Katrina reaches Category 3.
- 9:00 am CDT: officials in St. Charles, St. Tammany, and Plaquemines parishes order mandatory evacuation; Jefferson and St. Bernard do not.
- 4:00 pm CDT: in Louisiana, Contraflow begins, reversing traffic on inbound interstate lanes.
- 5:00 pm CDT: New Orleans Mayor C. Ray Nagin declares a state of emergency and issues a voluntary evacuation order. President Bush declares a state of emergency in Louisiana.
- 11:00 pm: the National Hurricane Center issues a warning that Katrina is moving west toward New Orleans.

SUNDAY, AUGUST 28, 2005
- 1:40 am: Hurricane Katrina reaches Category 4.
- 8:00 am: Hurricane Katrina reaches Category 5.
- 10:00 am CDT: Mandatory evacuation of New Orleans is announced. The National Weather service predicts devastating damage.

- 12:00 pm CDT: Louisiana Superdome is opened. President Bush declares a state of emergency in Mississippi and Alabama (and Florida a federal disaster area).

MONDAY, AUGUST 29, 2005
- 6:10 am CDT: as a Category 4 hurricane, Katrina makes landfall at Buras/Triumph, Louisiana.
- 8:00 am CDT: water is seen rising on both sides of the Industrial Canal in New Orleans, due to storm surge.
- 8:14 am CDT: the National Weather Service New Orleans office issues a flash flood warning for the Ninth Ward and Arabi.
- 9:00 am CDT: there is 6 to 8 feet of water in the Lower Ninth Ward in New Orleans. The eye of the hurricane passes over New Orleans.
- 10:00 am CDT: Hurricane Katrina makes landfall a third time as a Category 3 storm at Pearlington, Mississippi. Meanwhile, the storm rips two holes in the roof of the Superdome.
- 11:00 am CDT: there is approximately 10 feet of water in St. Bernard Parish. The 17th Street Canal levee is breached.
- 2:00 pm CDT: New Orleans officials confirm the breach of the 17th Street Canal levee.
- 3:00 pm CDT: Gov. Blanco orders 68 school buses into New Orleans to help evacuate survivors. FEMA director Michael Brown tells fire and rescue departments outside Louisiana, Alabama, and Mississippi not to respond to disaster areas without an explicit request for help from state or local governments. Meanwhile, The American Red Cross announces the largest mobilization in its history. President Bush declares major disaster areas in Alabama, Louisiana, and Mississippi.

TUESDAY, AUGUST 30, 2005
- 9:24 am PDT: the AP reports that President Bush will cut short his vacation to focus on Katrina issues.
- 12:00 pm CDT: Gov. Blanco commandeers hundreds of buses from across Louisiana to evacuate survivors stranded in New Orleans (an estimated 50,000 to 100,000).
- 10:00 pm CDT: Mayor Ray Nagin announces that the sandbagging of the 17th Street Canal has failed; 80 percent of the city is underwater.

WEDNESDAY, AUGUST 31, 2005
- Hurricane Katrina is downgraded to a tropical depression.
- The U.S. Navy moves ships and supplies into the gulf to support relief efforts.
- President Bush returns from vacation; Air Force One flies low over Louisiana.
- Mayor Ray Nagin orders almost the entire New Orleans police force to abandon search and rescue missions and begin to control the widespread looting; a curfew is placed in effect.
- 5:00 pm CDT: Gov. Blanco orders all of New Orleans to be evacuated.
- 11:00 pm: the National Hurricane Center announces that what was Hurricane Katrina has been completely absorbed by a frontal boundary in southeastern Canada. Heavy rainfall isolates north shore communities for several days.

THURSDAY, SEPTEMBER 1, 2005
- 2:00 am CDT: the first New Orleans evacuees arrive at the Astrodome in Houston.
- National Guard troops begin arriving at the Superdome; thousands of people there and at the Convention Center do not have food or water.
- Looting, carjacking and other violence spreads; Mayor Nagin calls the situation critical and issues "a desperate SOS."

- The New Orleans suburb of Gretna seals the Crescent City Connection bridge across the Mississippi River, turning back fleeing flood victims at gunpoint.

FRIDAY, SEPTEMBER 2, 2005
- President Bush tours the devastated Gulf Coast region.

SUNDAY, SEPTEMBER 4, 2005
- The evacuation of the Superdome is completed.

MONDAY, SEPTEMBER 5, 2005
- The 17th Street Canal levee breach is finally closed with rocks and sandbags.

FRIDAY, SEPTEMBER 9, 2005
- In a *20/20* interview, former Secretary of State Colin Powell criticizes the government's response, saying "When you look at those who weren't able to get out, it should have been a blinding flash of the obvious to everybody that when you order a mandatory evacuation, you can't expect everybody to evacuate on their own. These are people who don't have credit cards; only one in ten families at that economic level in New Orleans have a car. So it wasn't a racial thing, but poverty disproportionately affects African-Americans in this country. And it happened because they were poor."

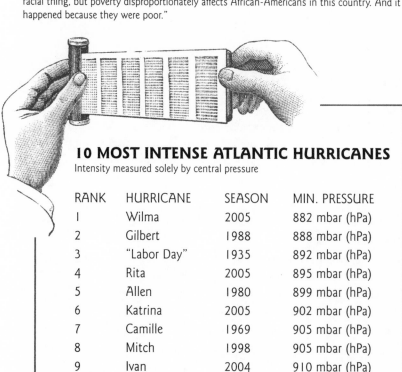

10 MOST INTENSE ATLANTIC HURRICANES
Intensity measured solely by central pressure

RANK	HURRICANE	SEASON	MIN. PRESSURE
1	Wilma	2005	882 mbar (hPa)
2	Gilbert	1988	888 mbar (hPa)
3	"Labor Day"	1935	892 mbar (hPa)
4	Rita	2005	895 mbar (hPa)
5	Allen	1980	899 mbar (hPa)
6	Katrina	2005	902 mbar (hPa)
7	Camille	1969	905 mbar (hPa)
8	Mitch	1998	905 mbar (hPa)
9	Ivan	2004	910 mbar (hPa)
10	Janet	1955	914 mbar (hPa)

Source: The Weather Channel

THE SOUTH'S WORST HURRICANES

HURRICANE	YEAR	CATEGORY
Katrina (LA/MS)	2005	4
Andrew (FL/LA)	1992	5
Hugo (SC)	1989	4
Camille (MS/LA/VA)	1969	5
New Orleans (LA)	1915	4
Last Island (LA)	1856	4

HURRICANE SEASON

The Atlantic hurricane season is June 1 through November 30, and produces about six hurricanes a year. Most don't make landfall, though—in a three-year period, roughly five will strike the coast.

HURRICANE-SPEAK

Tropical Disturbance – a thunderstorm in the tropics

Tropical Depression – system clouds and thunderstorms developing in tropical seas, with a defined circulation; winds are less than 38 mph

Tropical Storm – a step up from the depression: winds are 39–73 mph

Hurricane – an intense tropical storm with well-defined circulation and sustained winds of 74 mph and higher

Storm Surge – sea water pushed onshore by hurricane and tropical storm winds

Storm Tide – a combination of storm surge and the normal tide

Hurricane/Tropical Storm Watch – conditions are possible for the storm to develop in the specified area, usually within 36 hours.

Hurricane/Tropical Storm Warning – conditions are expected in the specified area, usually within 24 hours.

Category One – winds 74–95 mph; storm surge 4–5 ft. above normal

Category Two – winds 96–110 mph; storm surge 6–8 ft. above normal

Category Three – winds 111–130 mph; storm surge 9–12 ft. above normal

Category Four – winds 131–155 mph; storm surge 13–18 ft. above normal

Category Five – winds greater than 155 mph; storm surge greater than 18 ft.

Retired Hurricane Names

Agnes (1972)	David (1979)	Hattie (1961)	Lili (2002)
Alicia (1983)	Dennis (2005)	Hazel (1954)	Luis (1995)
Allen (1980)	Diana (1990)	Hilda (1964)	Marilyn (1995)
Allison (2001)	Diane (1955)	Hortense (1996)	Michelle (2001)
Andrew (1992)	Donna (1960)	Hugo (1989)	Mitch (1998)
Anita (1977)	Dora (1964)	Inez (1966)	Opal (1995)
Audrey (1957)	Edna (1968)	Ione (1955)	Rita (2005)
Betsy (1965)	Elena (1985)	Iris (2001)	Roxanne (1995)
Beulah (1967)	Eloise (1975)	Isabel (2003)	Stan (2005)
Bob (1991)	Fabian (2003)	Isidore (2002)	Wilma (2005)
Camille (1969)	Fifi (1974)	Ivan (2004)	
Carla (1961)	Flora (1963)	Janet (1955)	
Carmen (1974)	Floyd (1999)	Jeanne (2004)	
Carol (1954)	Fran (1996)	Joan (1988)	
Celia (1970)	Frances (2004)	Juan (2003)	
Cesar (1996)	Frederic (1979)	Katrina (2005)	
Charley (2004)	Georges (1998)	Keith (2000)	
Cleo (1964)	Gilbert (1988)	Klaus (1990)	
Connie (1955)	Gloria (1985)	Lenny (1999)	

BASIC HURRICANE SAFETY ACTIONS

- Know if you live in an evacuation area. Know your home's vulnerability to storm surge, flooding and wind. Have a written plan based on this knowledge.

- At the beginning of hurricane season (June 1), check your supplies, replace batteries, and use food stocks on a rotating basis.

- During hurricane season, monitor the tropics. Monitor NOAA Weather Radio.

- If a storm threatens, heed the advice from local authorities. Evacuate if ordered.

- Execute your family plan.

Source: National Ocean & Atmospheric Administration (NOAA),, U.S. Department of Commerce

BABY, IT'S COLD (HOT) OUTSIDE!

For some strange reason, we want to know just how miserably hot or bone-chilling cold it feels like. The heat index is the temperature the body *feels* when heat and humidity are combined. Similar to the heat index, wind chill measures the combined effect of cold air and wind to determine how cold it *feels*.

WIND CHILL CHART

WIND (MPH)	TEMPERATURE (°F)																	
Calm	40	35	30	25	20	15	10	5	0	-5	-10	-15	-20	-25	-30	-35	-40
5	36	31	25	19	13	7	1	-5	-11	-16	-22	-28	-34	-40	-46	-52	-57
10	34	27	21	15	9	3	-4	-10	-16	-22	-28	-35	-41	-47	-53	-59	-66
15	32	25	19	13	6	0	-7	-13	-19	-26	-32	-39	-45	-51	-58	-64	-71
20	30	24	17	11	4	-2	-9	-15	-22	-29	-35	-42	-48	-55	-61	-68	-74
25	29	23	16	9	3	-4	-11	-17	-24	-31	-37	-44	-51	-58	-64	-71	-78
30	28	22	15	8	1	-5	-12	-19	-26	-33	-39	-46	-53	-60	-67	-73	-80
35	28	21	14	7	0	-7	-14	-21	-27	-34	-41	-48	-55	-62	-69	-76	-82
40	27	20	13	6	-1	-8	-15	-22	-29	-36	-43	-50	-57	-64	-71	-78	-84
45	26	19	12	5	-2	-9	-16	-23	-30	-37	-44	-51	-58	-65	-72	-79	-86
50	26	19	12	4	-3	-10	-17	-24	-31	-38	-45	-52	-60	-67	-74	-81	-88
55	25	18	11	4	-3	-11	-18	-25	-32	-39	-46	-54	-61	-68	-75	-82	-89
60	25	17	10	3	-4	-11	-19	-26	-33	-40	-48	-55	-62	-69	-76	-84	-91

HEAT INDEX

Temperature (F) versus Relative Humidity (%)

F	90%	80%	70%	60%	50%	40%
80	85	84	82	81	80	79
85	101	96	92	90	86	84
90	121	113	105	99	94	90
95		133	122	113	105	98
100			142	129	118	109
105				148	133	121
110						135

Heat Index	Possible Heat Disorder
80 F—90 F	Fatigue possible with prolonged exposure and physical activity.
90 F—105 F	Sunstroke, heat cramps, and heat exhaustion possible.
105 F—130 F	Sunstroke, heat cramps, and heat exhaustion likely, and heat stroke possible.
130 F or greater	Heat stroke like with continued exposure.

THE MIGHTY MISSISSIPPI

*The Mississippi River plays such an important role in Southern conscious-
ness, we have to remind ourselves that the Big Muddy actually has its origins
far, far to the north, at Lake Itasca in Minnesota.*

FACTS ABOUT THE MISSISSIPPI

• It's the second-longest river in the United States (after the Missouri, which flows into the Mississippi)—and combined, they are the largest river system in North America.

• On its way south, the Mississippi flows through or borders ten states: Minnesota, Wisconsin, Iowa, Illinois, Missouri, Kentucky, Tennessee, Arkansas, Mississippi, and Louisiana.

• The lower Mississippi River switches course naturally about every 1,000 years or so.

• The distance from Lake Itasca to the mouth of the river below New Orleans is approximately 2,320 miles.

• A raindrop falling in Lake Itasca would take roughly 90 days to arrive at the Gulf of Mexico.

• North of St. Louis, there are a series of 29 locks and dams on the river, designed to maintain a deep enough channel to support commercial barge traffic. Most were built in the 1930s.

SIGNIFICANT SOUTHERN FLOODS

2005 • New Orleans • Aftermath of Hurricane Katrina
2005 • south Louisiana • Hurricane Rita
2001 • Houston • Tropical Storm Allison
1999 • North Carolina • Hurricane Floyd
1995 • south Louisiana and Mississippi • heavy rainfall
1985 • West Virginia • heavy rainfall
1983 • Mississippi • heavy rainfall
1977 • Toccoa, GA • Kelly Barnes Dam fails
1972 • West Virginia • Hurricane Agnes
1969 • West Virginia • Hurricane Camille
1965 • New Orleans • Hurricane Betsy
1957 • southwest Louisiana • storm surge from Hurricane Audrey
1927 • AR, IL, KY, LA, MS, TN • the Mississippi River floods

THE GREAT
FLOOD OF 1927

The Great Mississippi Flood of 1927 was the most destructive river flood in United States history. Heavy rainfall in the fall and winter of 1926 had swollen the river to its capacity, and as the spring approached, there was widespread concern that flooding would be of epic proportions.

It was. Melting snow at the headwaters and continued rains (New Orleans, for example, got fifteen inches of rain in one eighteen-hour period just before Easter) caused the river to rise. Up and down the Mississippi, communities raced to build up the height of the levees, pressing convicts and African-Americans into service, often at gunpoint, even though the U.S. Army Corps of Engineers had assured the public that the levees would hold.

They did not. On the morning of Good Friday, the rain started, setting records over several hundred thousand square miles; on Saturday morning, the first levee gave way at Cairo, Illinois. As the rains continued, the river broke through thirteen levees, killing more than a thousand and displacing almost a million people across six states. Over 26,000 square miles were covered by over thirty feet of floodwater, and at one point the Mississippi was 70 miles wide.

Horror stories were everywhere, including the over 13,000 people—almost all of them African-American—in the Greenville, Mississippi, area who gathered from area farms and evacuated to the crest of an unbroken levee, then were stranded there for days without food or clean water. Almost 300,000 African-Americans were forced to live in refugee camps for months, and many were coerced into relief efforts.

Flooding finally stopped in June, but the catastrophe ruined more than five million acres of farmland; many people, both black and white, left the land and never returned. More important, the disaster profoundly changed race relations, government, and society in the Mississippi River valley region. It brought Huey Long to power in Louisiana, and—due to then–Secretary of State, later president Herbert Hoover's broken promises—sparked the shift in shift in Southern African-American allegiance from the Republican to the Democratic Party.

The Largest **Quake** in United States History

Reelfoot Lake, a shallow natural lake in northwest Tennessee, was created during a series of three of the most powerful earthquakes in U.S. history, which were felt as far away as Quebec, Canada. Tradition says the lake formed when the Mississippi River flowed backwards, and that's not too far from the truth.

In the winter of 1811-12, terrified residents of New Madrid, Missouri, were abruptly awakened by violent shaking and a deafening roar. Trees were split and thrust into the air as the land buckled and rolled, shooting hundreds of waterspouts and sand upwards across the heaving landscape. Large areas of land sank and rose and rapids and waterfalls were created on bends of the Mississippi River. The small riverboat town of New Madrid just happened to be sitting astride three of the six fault segments in this area, which even today has more earthquakes than any other region east of the Rockies.

Landslides swept down steep bluffs as large areas of land were either uplifted or sank. The severe disruption of the mighty Mississippi caused a huge upstream wave, which surged against the strong current into a newly created depression, and Reelfoot Lake was born.

Reelfoot Lake is one of the greatest hunting and fishing preserves in the nation, and a naturalist's paradise. The lake encompasses 25,000 acres and is home to golden and American bald eagles and almost every kind of shore and wading bird. Cypress

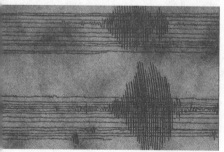

dominates the fringes of the lake, and the surrounding woodland is flush with trees, shrubs and flowering plants. Naturalist-guided tours are available year-round. Reelfoot Lake State Park is popular with canoeists, fishermen, hikers, and cyclists.

"I DON'T THINK WE'RE IN KANSAS (ER, KENTUCKY?) ANYMORE, TOTO"

Tornadoes are the deadliest storms on earth. Defined by the National Weather Service as "a violently rotating column of air in contact with the ground and a thunderstorm," they can occur in the presence of specific weather conditions, the primary one being a large, severe thunderstorm. Tornadoes often come in clusters. When weather conditions are right—large thunderstorms spreading for miles—the twisters peel themselves off over a wide area and over a period of many hours, which is why a particular storm system is often referred to as a tornado outbreak. Peak season in the South is March through May.

Tornado Myths

Don't believe it! All of these statements are false.

1. A highway bridge underpass makes a safe haven if you're on the road.
2. Open the windows to equalize air pressure so the house won't explode.
3. The southwest corner of the building is the safest.
4. You can see a tornado coming in time to take shelter.
5. Tornadoes can't cross rivers or other bodies of water.
6. Tornadoes can't cross steep terrain.
7. Tornadoes can't survive in an urban area.
8. You can outdrive a tornado.

THE SOUTH'S DEADLIEST TORNADOES

DATE	PLACE	DEATHS
Mar. 21-22, 1932	Deep South Outbreak	330
May 6, 1840	Natchez, MS	317
Apr. 3, 1974	Supertornado (OH, KY, AL, IN)*	315
Apr. 5, 1936	Tupelo, MS*	216
Mar. 21-22, 1952	Tennessee/Arkansas*	208
Apr. 6, 1936	Gainesville, GA*	203
Mar. 16, 1942	Southern U.S.	148
Apr. 24, 1908	Amite LA, Purvis MS	143
Feb. 21, 1971	Mississippi Delta Outbreak*	119
Apr. 22-23, 1883	Southeastern U.S.	109
Nov. 25-26, 1926	Southern U.S.	107
Jun. 23, 1944	Shinnston WV	100
Jun. 1, 1903	Gainesville, Holland GA	98
Apr. 24, 1908	Natchez, MS	91
Apr. 15-16, 1921	Southeastern U.S.	90
Apr. 20, 1920	Starkville, MS, Waco, AL	88
Mar. 30-31, 1933	Southeastern U.S.	87
Mar. 27, 1890	Louisville, KY	76
May 1, 1875	Southeastern U.S.	58
Mar. 28, 1984	Carolinas Outbreak	57

* indicates an F5 tornado

TORNADO WARNING SIGNS

TIME BEFORE TORNADO ARRIVES / WARNING SIGN
- 1–6 HRS / ROTATING THUNDERHEAD TURBULENCE
- 1–90 MIN / HANGING CLOUD FORMATIONS ON LEADING EDGE OF STORM FRONT
- 1–45 MIN / DARK, GREENISH SKY
- 0–30 MIN / CONTINUOUS LIGHTNING
- 0–20 MIN / LARGE HAIL
- 0–15 MIN / WALL CLOUD
- 0–10 MIN / LOUD ROAR, ABOVE THE NOISE OF A THUNDERSTORM
- 0–3 MIN / FLYING DEBRIS
- 0–60 SEC / BUZZING BEES NOISE
- 0–20 SEC / SUDDEN WINDOW BREAKAGE
- 0–5 SEC / SUDDEN CALM

WEATHER AVERAGES

ASHEVILLE, NC

Average Temperature (Years on Record: 23)

	YEAR	Jan.	Feb.	Mar.	Apr.	May	Jun.	Jul.	Aug.	Sep.	Oct.	Nov.	Dec.
°F	56	38	41	46	57	65	71	74	73	67	57	47	39

Average Precipitation (Years on Record: 23)

	YEAR	Jan.	Feb.	Mar.	Apr.	May	Jun.	Jul.	Aug.	Sep.	Oct.	Nov.	Dec.
in.	38.1	2.6	3.1	4	3.3	2.9	3.5	3.4	4	3.1	2.7	2.6	2.7

Average Snowfall (Years on Record: 29)

	YEAR	Jan.	Feb.	Mar.	Apr.	May	Jun.	Jul.	Aug.	Sep.	Oct.	Nov.	Dec.
in.	15.6	4.6	4.6	3	0.7	---	---	---	---	---	---	0.7	2

Average Possibility of Sunshine (Years on Record: 29)

	YEAR	Jan.	Feb.	Mar.	Apr.	May	Jun.	Jul.	Aug.	Sep.	Oct.	Nov.	Dec.
%	59	55	59	60	65	61	63	60	54	56	61	58	55

Average Number of Clear Days (Years on Record: 29)

	YEAR	Jan.	Feb.	Mar.	Apr.	May	Jun.	Jul.	Aug.	Sep.	Oct.	Nov.	Dec.
Days	101	9	9	9	10	7	6	5	5	7	12	11	10

Average Number of Cloudy Days (Years on Record: 2)

	YEAR	Jan.	Feb.	Mar.	Apr.	May	Jun.	Jul.	Aug.	Sep.	Oct.	Nov.	Dec.
Days	151	14	13	14	12	14	12	12	12	12	11	12	14

Average Number of Partly Cloudy Days (Years on Record: 29)

	YEAR	Jan.	Feb.	Mar.	Apr.	May	Jun.	Jul.	Aug.	Sep.	Oct.	Nov.	Dec.
Days	113	8	6	8	8	10	12	14	14	11	8	7	7

Average Number of Rainy Days (Years on Record: 29)

	YEAR	Jan.	Feb.	Mar.	Apr.	May	Jun.	Jul.	Aug.	Sep.	Oct.	Nov.	Dec.
Days	125	10	9	11	9	12	11	12	13	10	8	9	10

ATHENS, GA

Average Temperature (Years on Record: 41)

	YEAR	Jan.	Feb.	Mar.	Apr.	May	Jun.	Jul.	Aug.	Sep.	Oct.	Nov.	Dec.
°F	62	42	46	53	62	70	77	80	79	73	62	53	45

Average Precipitation (Years on Record: 41)

	YEAR	Jan.	Feb.	Mar.	Apr.	May	Jun.	Jul.	Aug.	Sep.	Oct.	Nov.	Dec.
in.	50.2	4.6	4.5	5.5	3.8	4.3	4.1	5	3.8	3.6	3.4	3.7	3.8

ATHENS, GA, CONT.

Average Snowfall   (Years on Record: 50)

	YEAR	Jan.	Feb.	Mar.	Apr.	May	Jun.	Jul.	Aug.	Sep.	Oct.	Nov.	Dec.
in.	2.4	0.9	0.7	0.5	---	---	---	---	---	---	---	0.1	0.2

Average Number of Clear Days   (Years on Record: 50)

	YEAR	Jan.	Feb.	Mar.	Apr.	May	Jun.	Jul.	Aug.	Sep.	Oct.	Nov.	Dec.
Days	113	9	9	9	10	9	8	7	8	10	14	12	10

Average Number of Rainy Days   (Years on Record: 50)

	YEAR	Jan.	Feb.	Mar.	Apr.	May	Jun.	Jul.	Aug.	Sep.	Oct.	Nov.	Dec.
Days	110	11	9	11	8	9	9	11	9	8	7	8	10

ATLANTA, GA

Average Temperature   (Years on Record: 50)

	YEAR	Jan.	Feb.	Mar.	Apr.	May	Jun.	Jul.	Aug.	Sep.	Oct.	Nov.	Dec.
°F	62	43	46	53	62	70	77	79	79	73	63	53	45

Average Precipitation   (Years on Record: 50)

	YEAR	Jan.	Feb.	Mar.	Apr.	May	Jun.	Jul.	Aug.	Sep.	Oct.	Nov.	Dec.
in.	50.3	4.7	4.6	5.6	4.1	4	3.7	5.3	3.7	3.6	3	4	4.1

Average Snowfall   (Years on Record: 59)

	YEAR	Jan.	Feb.	Mar.	Apr.	May	Jun.	Jul.	Aug.	Sep.	Oct.	Nov.	Dec.
in.	2	0.9	0.5	0.4	---	---	---	---	---	---	---	---	0.2

Average Possibility of Sunshine   (Years on Record: 58)

	YEAR	Jan.	Feb.	Mar.	Apr.	May	Jun.	Jul.	Aug.	Sep.	Oct.	Nov.	Dec.
%	61	49	54	58	66	68	67	63	64	63	67	58	50

Average Number of Rainy Days   (Years on Record: 59)

	YEAR	Jan.	Feb.	Mar.	Apr.	May	Jun.	Jul.	Aug.	Sep.	Oct.	Nov.	Dec.
Days	115	11	10	11	9	9	10	12	10	8	6	8	10

AUGUSTA, GA

Average Temperature   (Years on Record: 47)

	YEAR	Jan.	Feb.	Mar.	Apr.	May	Jun.	Jul.	Aug.	Sep.	Oct.	Nov.	Dec.
°F	64	45	49	55	63	71	78	81	80	75	64	55	47

Average Precipitation   (Years on Record: 47)

	YEAR	Jan.	Feb.	Mar.	Apr.	May	Jun.	Jul.	Aug.	Sep.	Oct.	Nov.	Dec.
in.	43.8	4	4.1	4.6	3.2	3.5	3.9	4.5	4.3	3.2	2.8	2.3	3.2

Average Snowfall   (Years on Record: 43)

	YEAR	Jan.	Feb.	Mar.	Apr.	May	Jun.	Jul.	Aug.	Sep.	Oct.	Nov.	Dec.
in.	1.2	0.3	0.8	---	---	---	---	---	---	---	---	---	0.1

Average Number of Clear Days (Years on Record: 43)

YEAR	Jan.	Feb.	Mar.	Apr.	May	Jun.	Jul.	Aug.	Sep.	Oct.	Nov.	Dec.
Days 112	9	9	9	11	8	8	6	7	9	14	12	10

Average Number of Rainy Days (Years on Record: 43)

YEAR	Jan.	Feb.	Mar.	Apr.	May	Jun.	Jul.	Aug.	Sep.	Oct.	Nov.	Dec.
Days 107	10	9	10	8	9	9	11	10	7	6	7	9

BATON ROUGE, LA

Average Temperature (Years on Record: 48)

YEAR	Jan.	Feb.	Mar.	Apr.	May	Jun.	Jul.	Aug.	Sep.	Oct.	Nov.	Dec.
°F 68	51	54	61	68	75	81	82	82	78	69	59	53

Average Precipitation (Years on Record: 48)

YEAR	Jan.	Feb.	Mar.	Apr.	May	Jun.	Jul.	Aug.	Sep.	Oct.	Nov.	Dec.
in. 58.5	4.9	5.1	4.8	5.5	5	4.4	6.6	5.4	4.1	3.1	4.2	5.3

Average Number of Clear Days (Years on Record: 42)

YEAR	Jan.	Feb.	Mar.	Apr.	May	Jun.	Jul.	Aug.	Sep.	Oct.	Nov.	Dec.
Days 99	7	7	8	8	8	7	5	7	9	15	9	8

Average Number of Rainy Days (Years on Record: 42)

YEAR	Jan.	Feb.	Mar.	Apr.	May	Jun.	Jul.	Aug.	Sep.	Oct.	Nov.	Dec.
Days 110	10	9	9	7	8	10	13	12	9	5	8	10

BIRMINGHAM, AL

Average Temperature (Years on Record:

YEAR	Jan.	Feb.	Mar.	Apr.	May	Jun.	Jul.	Aug.	Sep.	Oct.	Nov.	Dec.
°F 63	43	4754		63	70	77	80	80	74	63	53	46

Average Precipitation (Years on Record: 48)

YEAR	Jan.	Feb.	Mar.	Apr.	May	Jun.	Jul.	Aug.	Sep.	Oct.	Nov.	Dec.
in. 53.5	5	4.8	5.9	4.6	4.4	3.8	5.1	3.8	4.1	2.9	4.3	4.8

Average Snowfall (Years on Record: 11)

YEAR	Jan.	Feb.	Mar.	Apr.	May	Jun.	Jul.	Aug.	Sep.	Oct.	Nov.	Dec.
in. 1.9	0.8	0.1	0.5	0.5	---	---	---	---	---	---	---	---

Average Possibility of Sunshine (Years on Record: 10)

YEAR	Jan.	Feb.	Mar.	Apr.	May	Jun.	Jul.	Aug.	Sep.	Oct.	Nov.	Dec.
% 57	48	48	62	61	64	63	60	62	57	63	49	52

Average Number of Rainy Days (Years on Record: 11)

YEAR	Jan.	Feb.	Mar.	Apr.	May	Jun.	Jul.	Aug.	Sep.	Oct.	Nov.	Dec.
Days 117	10	10	11	9	10	9	12	10	9	8	10	9

BRISTOL, TN

Average Temperature (Years on Record: 48)

	YEAR	Jan.	Feb.	Mar.	Apr.	May	Jun.	Jul.	Aug.	Sep.	Oct.	Nov.	Dec.
°F	56	36	39	47	56	64	72	75	74	68	57	47	39

Average Precipitation (Years on Record: 48)

	YEAR	Jan.	Feb.	Mar.	Apr.	May	Jun.	Jul.	Aug.	Sep.	Oct.	Nov.	Dec.
in.	41.5	3.4	3.6	4	3.3	3.8	3.5	4.4	3.4	3	2.4	3.1	3.5

Average Snowfall (Years on Record: 56)

	YEAR	Jan.	Feb.	Mar.	Apr.	May	Jun.	Jul.	Aug.	Sep.	Oct.	Nov.	Dec.
in.	15.7	5.1	4.3	2.3	0.4	---	---	---	---	---	---	1	2.6

Average Number of Clear Days (Years on Record: 56)

	YEAR	Jan.	Feb.	Mar.	Apr.	May	Jun.	Jul.	Aug.	Sep.	Oct.	Nov.	Dec.
Days	89	6	6	6	7	7	6	6	7	9	12	9	7

Average Number of Rainy Days (Years on Record: 48)

	YEAR	Jan.	Feb.	Mar.	Apr.	May	Jun.	Jul.	Aug.	Sep.	Oct.	Nov.	Dec.
Days	133	14	12	13	11	12	11	12	10	8	8	10	12

CAPE HATTERAS, NC

Average Temperature (Years on Record: 39)

	YEAR	Jan.	Feb.	Mar.	Apr.	May	Jun.	Jul.	Aug.	Sep.	Oct.	Nov.	Dec.
°F	63	45	46	52	60	67	75	79	79	75	66	58	49

Average Precipitation (Years on Record: 39)

	YEAR	Jan.	Feb.	Mar.	Apr.	May	Jun.	Jul.	Aug.	Sep.	Oct.	Nov.	Dec.
in.	56.9	5.6	4.1	4.6	3.2	3.8	4.2	4.9	6.4	5.3	5.3	4.9	4.5

Average Snowfall (Years on Record: 36)

	YEAR	Jan.	Feb.	Mar.	Apr.	May	Jun.	Jul.	Aug.	Sep.	Oct.	Nov.	Dec.
in.	2	0.4	0.6	0.4	---	---	---	---	---	---	---	---	0.6

Average Number of Rainy Days (Years on Record: 36)

	YEAR	Jan.	Feb.	Mar.	Apr.	May	Jun.	Jul.	Aug.	Sep.	Oct.	Nov.	Dec.
Days	120	11	10	11	9	10	9	12	11	9	9	9	10

CHARLESTON, SC

Average Temperature (Years on Record: 50)

	YEAR	Jan.	Feb.	Mar.	Apr.	May	Jun.	Jul.	Aug.	Sep.	Oct.	Nov.	Dec.
°F	66	49	51	57	65	73	78	81	81	76	67	58	51

Average Precipitation (Years on Record: 50)

	YEAR	Jan.	Feb.	Mar.	Apr.	May	Jun.	Jul.	Aug.	Sep.	Oct.	Nov.	Dec.
in.	52.1	3.5	3.1	4.4	2.8	4.1	6	7.2	6.9	5.6	3.1	2.5	3.1

Average Number of Rainy Days (Years on Record: 20)

	YEAR	Jan.	Feb.	Mar.	Apr.	May	Jun.	Jul.	Aug.	Sep.	Oct.	Nov.	Dec.
Days	106	10	8	9	7	8	10	10	12	10	6	8	9

CHARLOTTE, NC

Average Temperature (Years on Record: 48)

	YEAR	Jan.	Feb.	Mar.	Apr.	May	Jun.	Jul.	Aug.	Sep.	Oct.	Nov.	Dec.
°F	61	41	44	51	61	69	76	80	78	72	61	52	43

Average Precipitation (Years on Record: 48)

	YEAR	Jan.	Feb.	Mar.	Apr.	May	Jun.	Jul.	Aug.	Sep.	Oct.	Nov.	Dec.
in.	43	3.7	3.7	4.6	3	3.6	3.5	3.8	4.1	3.3	3.2	3.1	3.3

Average Snowfall (Years on Record: 54)

	YEAR	Jan.	Feb.	Mar.	Apr.	May	Jun.	Jul.	Aug.	Sep.	Oct.	Nov.	Dec.
in.	5.5	2	1.7	1.2	---	---	---	---	---	---	---	0.1	0.5

Average Number of Clear Days (Years on Record: 45)

	YEAR	Jan.	Feb.	Mar.	Apr.	May	Jun.	Jul.	Aug.	Sep.	Oct.	Nov.	Dec.
Days	111	9	8	9	10	8	8	7	7	9	13	12	10

Average Number of Rainy Days (Years on Record: 54)

	YEAR	Jan.	Feb.	Mar.	Apr.	May	Jun.	Jul.	Aug.	Sep.	Oct.	Nov.	Dec.
Days	111	10	10	11	9	10	9	11	10	7	7	8	10

CHATTANOOGA, TN

Average Temperature (Years on Record: 48)

	YEAR	Jan.	Feb.	Mar.	Apr.	May	Jun.	Jul.	Aug.	Sep.	Oct.	Nov.	Dec.
°F	60	40	43	51	60	68	76	79	78	72	61	50	42

Average Precipitation (Years on Record: 48)

	YEAR	Jan.	Feb.	Mar.	Apr.	May	Jun.	Jul.	Aug.	Sep.	Oct.	Nov.	Dec.
in.	53.6	5.2	5.1	6	4.3	4	3.7	4.8	3.5	4.1	3.2	4.5	5.1

Average Snowfall (Years on Record: 63)

	YEAR	Jan.	Feb.	Mar.	Apr.	May	Jun.	Jul.	Aug.	Sep.	Oct.	Nov.	Dec.
in.	4.4	1.8	1.2	0.7	0.1	---	---	---	---	---	---	---	0.6

Average Number of Clear Days (Years on Record: 63)

	YEAR	Jan.	Feb.	Mar.	Apr.	May	Jun.	Jul.	Aug.	Sep.	Oct.	Nov.	Dec.
Days	105	7	7	8	9	9	8	7	8	10	13	10	8

Average Number of Rainy Days (Years on Record: 63)

	YEAR	Jan.	Feb.	Mar.	Apr.	May	Jun.	Jul.	Aug.	Sep.	Oct.	Nov.	Dec.
Days	120	12	10	12	10	10	10	12	10	8	7	9	11

COLUMBUS, GA

Average Temperature   (Years on Record: 48)

	YEAR	Jan.	Feb.	Mar.	Apr.	May	Jun.	Jul.	Aug.	Sep.	Oct.	Nov.	Dec.
°F	65	47	50	57	65	72	79	82	81	76	66	56	49

Average Precipitation   (Years on Record: 48)

	YEAR	Jan.	Feb.	Mar.	Apr.	May	Jun.	Jul.	Aug.	Sep.	Oct.	Nov.	Dec.
in.	50.3	4.3	4.7	5.8	4.2	4	3.8	5.7	4	3.2	2.3	3.6	4.7

Average Snowfall   (Years on Record: 48)

	YEAR	Jan.	Feb.	Mar.	Apr.	May	Jun.	Jul.	Aug.	Sep.	Oct.	Nov.	Dec.
in.	0.5	0.1	0.3	0.1	---	---	---	---	---	---	---	---	---

Average Number of Clear Days   (Years on Record: 48)

	YEAR	Jan.	Feb.	Mar.	Apr.	May	Jun.	Jul.	Aug.	Sep.	Oct.	Nov.	Dec.
Days	110	8	8	9	10	9	8	6	8	10	14	12	9

Average Number of Rainy Days   (Years on Record: 48)

	YEAR	Jan.	Feb.	Mar.	Apr.	May	Jun.	Jul.	Aug.	Sep.	Oct.	Nov.	Dec.
Days	110	10	10	10	8	8	9	13	10	8	5	8	10

GREENSBORO, NC

Average Temperature   (Years on Record: 48)

	YEAR	Jan.	Feb.	Mar.	Apr.	May	Jun.	Jul.	Aug.	Sep.	Oct.	Nov.	Dec.
°F	58	38	41	49	58	67	74	78	76	70	59	49	41

Average Precipitation   (Years on Record: 48)

	YEAR	Jan.	Feb.	Mar.	Apr.	May	Jun.	Jul.	Aug.	Sep.	Oct.	Nov.	Dec.
in.	42.3	3.3	3.3	3.8	3.2	3.6	3.8	4.4	4.1	3.3	3.4	2.9	3.2

Average Snowfall   (Years on Record: 65)

	YEAR	Jan.	Feb.	Mar.	Apr.	May	Jun.	Jul.	Aug.	Sep.	Oct.	Nov.	Dec.
in.	8.6	3.1	2.5	1.7	---	---	---	---	---	---	---	0.1	1.2

Average Number of Clear Days   (Years on Record: 65)

	YEAR	Jan.	Feb.	Mar.	Apr.	May	Jun.	Jul.	Aug.	Sep.	Oct.	Nov.	Dec.
Days	109	9	9	9	9	8	7	6	7	10	14	11	10

Average Number of Rainy Days   (Years on Record: 65)

	YEAR	Jan.	Feb.	Mar.	Apr.	May	Jun.	Jul.	Aug.	Sep.	Oct.	Nov.	Dec.
Days	116	10	10	11	9	10	10	12	10	8	7	8	9

WINSTON-SALEM

Average Temperature   (Years on Record: 17)

	YEAR	Jan.	Feb.	Mar.	Apr.	May	Jun.	Jul.	Aug.	Sep.	Oct.	Nov.	Dec.
°F	57	39	41	46	57	66	73	77	75	69	59	48	39

Average Precipitation (Years on Record: 17)

	YEAR	Jan.	Feb.	Mar.	Apr.	May	Jun.	Jul.	Aug.	Sep.	Oct.	Nov.	Dec.
in.	44.3	3.4	3.6	4.2	3.7	3.9	4.1	4.2	4.2	3.2	3.2	2.9	3.6

GREENVILLE, NC

Average Temperature (Years on Record: 31)

	YEAR	Jan.	Feb.	Mar.	Apr.	May	Jun.	Jul.	Aug.	Sep.	Oct.	Nov.	Dec.
°F	61	43	45	51	60	69	76	79	78	73	63	52	44

Average Precipitation (Years on Record: 64)

	YEAR	Jan.	Feb.	Mar.	Apr.	May	Jun.	Jul.	Aug.	Sep.	Oct.	Nov.	Dec.
in.	48.6	3.4	3.6	3.8	3.6	3.7	4.8	6.6	5.4	4.9	3	2.6	3.3

Average Snowfall (Years on Record: 7)

	YEAR	Jan.	Feb.	Mar.	Apr.	May	Jun.	Jul.	Aug.	Sep.	Oct.	Nov.	Dec.
in.	1.4	0.7	0.2	0.3	---	---	---	---	---	---	---	---	0.2

Average Number of Rainy Days (Years on Record: 64)

	YEAR	Jan.	Feb.	Mar.	Apr.	May	Jun.	Jul.	Aug.	Sep.	Oct.	Nov.	Dec.
Days	82	6.7	6.9	6.7	6.6	6.6	7.6	9.2	8.1	7.5	5	4.5	6.6

HUNTSVILLE, AL

Average Temperature (Years on Record: 37)

	YEAR	Jan.	Feb.	Mar.	Apr.	May	Jun.	Jul.	Aug.	Sep.	Oct.	Nov.	Dec.
°F	61	39	44	52	61	69	76	80	79	73	62	51	43

Average Precipitation (Years on Record: 37)

	YEAR	Jan.	Feb.	Mar.	Apr.	May	Jun.	Jul.	Aug.	Sep.	Oct.	Nov.	Dec.
in.	56.8	5	5	6.6	4.8	5.1	4.3	4.6	3.5	4.1	3.3	4.7	5.7

Average Snowfall (Years on Record: 26)

	YEAR	Jan.	Feb.	Mar.	Apr.	May	Jun.	Jul.	Aug.	Sep.	Oct.	Nov.	Dec.
in.	2.8	1.5	0.7	0.4	---	---	---	---	---	---	---	---	0.2

Average Number of Clear Days (Years on Record: 26)

	YEAR	Jan.	Feb.	Mar.	Apr.	May	Jun.	Jul.	Aug.	Sep.	Oct.	Nov.	Dec.
Days	100	7	7	7	9	8	8	7	9	9	12	9	7

Average Number of Rainy Days (Years on Record: 26)

	YEAR	Jan.	Feb.	Mar.	Apr.	May	Jun.	Jul.	Aug.	Sep.	Oct.	Nov.	Dec.
Days	117	11	10	12	10	11	9	10	9	9	7	10	11

JACKSON, MS

Average Temperature (Years on Record: 32)

	YEAR	Jan.	Feb.	Mar.	Apr.	May	Jun.	Jul.	Aug.	Sep.	Oct.	Nov.	Dec.
°F	65	45	49	57	65	72	79	82	81	76	65	56	49

JACKSON, MS., CONT.

Average Precipitation (Years on Record: 32)

	YEAR	Jan.	Feb.	Mar.	Apr.	May	Jun.	Jul.	Aug.	Sep.	Oct.	Nov.	Dec.
in.	55.4	5.1	4.6	5.7	5.9	5.2	3.3	4.6	3.9	3.5	3.4	4.7	5.6

Average Snowfall (Years on Record: 30)

	YEAR	Jan.	Feb.	Mar.	Apr.	May	Jun.	Jul.	Aug.	Sep.	Oct.	Nov.	Dec.
in.	0.9	0.5	0.2	0.2	---	---	---	---	---	---	---	---	---

Average Number of Clear Days (Years on Record: 30)

	YEAR	Jan.	Feb.	Mar.	Apr.	May	Jun.	Jul.	Aug.	Sep.	Oct.	Nov.	Dec.
Days	111	8	8	9	10	8	9	8	9	10	15	10	9

Average Number of Rainy Days (Years on Record: 30)

	YEAR	Jan.	Feb.	Mar.	Apr.	May	Jun.	Jul.	Aug.	Sep.	Oct.	Nov.	Dec.
Days	110	11	9	10	9	10	8	10	10	8	6	8	10

KNOXVILLE, TN

Average Temperature (Years on Record: 48)

	YEAR	Jan.	Feb.	Mar.	Apr.	May	Jun.	Jul.	Aug.	Sep.	Oct.	Nov.	Dec.
°F	59	38	42	50	59	67	75	78	77	71	60	49	41

Average Precipitation (Years on Record: 48)

	YEAR	Jan.	Feb.	Mar.	Apr.	May	Jun.	Jul.	Aug.	Sep.	Oct.	Nov.	Dec.
in.	47.1	4.5	4.4	5.1	3.6	3.9	3.8	4.4	3.2	2.9	2.7	3.9	4.6

Average Snowfall (Years on Record: 51)

	YEAR	Jan.	Feb.	Mar.	Apr.	May	Jun.	Jul.	Aug.	Sep.	Oct.	Nov.	Dec.
in.	11.9	3.9	3.6	1.8	0.4	---	---	---	---	---	---	0.6	1.6

Average Number of Clear Days (Years on Record: 51)

	YEAR	Jan.	Feb.	Mar.	Apr.	May	Jun.	Jul.	Aug.	Sep.	Oct.	Nov.	Dec.
Days	97	6	7	7	8	8	8	7	9	9	12	9	7

Average Number of Rainy Days (Years on Record: 51)

	YEAR	Jan.	Feb.	Mar.	Apr.	May	Jun.	Jul.	Aug.	Sep.	Oct.	Nov.	Dec.
Days	126	12	11	13	11	11	10	11	9	8	8	10	11

LAKE CHARLES, LA

Average Temperature (Years on Record: 34)

	YEAR	Jan.	Feb.	Mar.	Apr.	May	Jun.	Jul.	Aug.	Sep.	Oct.	Nov.	Dec.
°F	68	51	54	61	69	75	81	83	82	78	70	61	54

Average Precipitation (Years on Record: 34)

	YEAR	Jan.	Feb.	Mar.	Apr.	May	Jun.	Jul.	Aug.	Sep.	Oct.	Nov.	Dec.
in.	55.6	5.1	3.4	3.4	3.7	5.4	5.6	5.1	5.3	5.4	3.9	4.4	4.9

Average Number of Clear Days (Years on Record: 32)

	YEAR	Jan.	Feb.	Mar.	Apr.	May	Jun.	Jul.	Aug.	Sep.	Oct.	Nov.	Dec.
Days	98	7	8	7	7	7	8	6	7	9	13	10	8

Average Number of Rainy Days (Years on Record: 32)

YEAR	Jan.	Feb.	Mar.	Apr.	May	Jun.	Jul.	Aug.	Sep.	Oct.	Nov.	Dec.
Days	103	10	8	8	7	8	9	11	11	9	6	8	9

LITTLE ROCK, AR

Average Temperature (Years on Record: 48)

	YEAR	Jan.	Feb.	Mar.	Apr.	May	Jun.	Jul.	Aug.	Sep.	Oct.	Nov.	Dec.
°F	62	40	45	53	63	71	79	82	81	74	63	52	44

Average Precipitation (Years on Record: 48)

	YEAR	Jan.	Feb.	Mar.	Apr.	May	Jun.	Jul.	Aug.	Sep.	Oct.	Nov.	Dec.
in.	50.5	4.1	4	4.8	5.3	5.2	3.6	3.5	3.2	3.8	3.6	4.9	4.4

Average Snowfall (Years on Record: 51)

	YEAR	Jan.	Feb.	Mar.	Apr.	May	Jun.	Jul.	Aug.	Sep.	Oct.	Nov.	Dec.
in.	5.1	2.3	1.4	0.5	---	---	---	---	---	---	---	0.2	0.7

Average Number of Clear Days (Years on Record: 35)

	YEAR	Jan.	Feb.	Mar.	Apr.	May	Jun.	Jul.	Aug.	Sep.	Oct.	Nov.	Dec.
Days	119	9	9	9	9	9	9	9	12	11	14	11	9

Average Number of Rainy Days (Years on Record: 51)

	YEAR	Jan.	Feb.	Mar.	Apr.	May	Jun.	Jul.	Aug.	Sep.	Oct.	Nov.	Dec.
Days	105	10	9	10	10	10	8	8	7	7	7	8	9

LOUISVILLE, KY

Average Temperature (Years on Record: 48)

	YEAR	Jan.	Feb.	Mar.	Apr.	May	Jun.	Jul.	Aug.	Sep.	Oct.	Nov.	Dec.
°F	57	33	37	46	57	66	74	78	77	70	58	47	37

Average Precipitation (Years on Record: 48)

	YEAR	Jan.	Feb.	Mar.	Apr.	May	Jun.	Jul.	Aug.	Sep.	Oct.	Nov.	Dec.
in.	43.6	3.4	3.4	4.5	4	4.5	3.6	4.2	3.3	3	2.6	3.7	3.5

Average Snowfall (Years on Record: 46)

	YEAR	Jan.	Feb.	Mar.	Apr.	May	Jun.	Jul.	Aug.	Sep.	Oct.	Nov.	Dec.
in.	16.2	5.1	4.5	3.2	0.1	---	---	---	---	---	0.1	1	2.2

Average Number of Clear Days (Years on Record: 46)

	YEAR	Jan.	Feb.	Mar.	Apr.	May	Jun.	Jul.	Aug.	Sep.	Oct.	Nov.	Dec.
Days	93	6	6	6	6	8	8	8	10	10	11	7	6

Average Number of Rainy Days (Years on Record: 46)

	YEAR	Jan.	Feb.	Mar.	Apr.	May	Jun.	Jul.	Aug.	Sep.	Oct.	Nov.	Dec.
Days	125	11	11	13	12	12	10	11	8	8	8	10	11

MACON, GA

Average Temperature	(Years on Record: 47)											
	YEAR	Jan.	Feb.	Mar.	Apr.	May	Jun.	Jul.	Aug.	Sep.	Oct.	Nov.	Dec.
°F	65	47	50	57	65	73	79	82	81	76	66	56	49

Average Precipitation	(Years on Record: 47)											
	YEAR	Jan.	Feb.	Mar.	Apr.	May	Jun.	Jul.	Aug.	Sep.	Oct.	Nov.	Dec.
in.	45.1	4.2	4.8	4.9	3.3	3.4	3.7	4.9	3.8	2.9	2.4	2.6	4.1

Average Snowfall	(Years on Record: 45)											
	YEAR	Jan.	Feb.	Mar.	Apr.	May	Jun.	Jul.	Aug.	Sep.	Oct.	Nov.	Dec.
in.	1	0.3	0.6	0.1	---	---	---	---	---	---	---	---	---

Average Number of Clear Days	(Years on Record: 45)											
	YEAR	Jan.	Feb.	Mar.	Apr.	May	Jun.	Jul.	Aug.	Sep.	Oct.	Nov.	Dec.
Days	112	8	8	9	11	9	8	6	9	9	14	12	9

Average Number of Rainy Days	(Years on Record: 45)											
	YEAR	Jan.	Feb.	Mar.	Apr.	May	Jun.	Jul.	Aug.	Sep.	Oct.	Nov.	Dec.
Days	110	11	10	10	7	9	10	13	11	8	6	7	9

MEMPHIS, TN

Average Temperature	(Years on Record: 48)											
	YEAR	Jan.	Feb.	Mar.	Apr.	May	Jun.	Jul.	Aug.	Sep.	Oct.	Nov.	Dec.
°F	62	40	45	53	63	71	79	83	81	74	63	52	44

Average Precipitation	(Years on Record: 48)											
	YEAR	Jan.	Feb.	Mar.	Apr.	May	Jun.	Jul.	Aug.	Sep.	Oct.	Nov.	Dec.
in.	52.4	4.7	4.5	5.2	5.6	4.9	3.9	3.9	3.4	3.2	2.9	4.8	5.3

Average Snowfall	(Years on Record: 43)											
	YEAR	Jan.	Feb.	Mar.	Apr.	May	Jun.	Jul.	Aug.	Sep.	Oct.	Nov.	Dec.
in.	5.1	2.3	1.3	0.8	---	---	---	---	---	---	---	0.1	0.6

Average Number of Clear Days	(Years on Record: 41)											
	YEAR	Jan.	Feb.	Mar.	Apr.	May	Jun.	Jul.	Aug.	Sep.	Oct.	Nov.	Dec.
Days	118	8	8	8	9	8	10	10	11	12	14	10	9

Average Number of Rainy Days	(Years on Record: 43)											
	YEAR	Jan.	Feb.	Mar.	Apr.	May	Jun.	Jul.	Aug.	Sep.	Oct.	Nov.	Dec.
Days	107	10	9	11	10	9	9	9	8	7	6	9	10

MERIDIAN, MS

Average Temperature	Years on Record: 48											
	YEAR	Jan.	Feb.	Mar.	Apr.	May	Jun.	Jul.	Aug.	Sep.	Oct.	Nov.	Dec.
°F	65	46	50	57	65	72	79	82	81	76	65	55	49

Average Precipitation (Years on Record: 48)

	YEAR	Jan.	Feb.	Mar.	Apr.	May	Jun.	Jul.	Aug.	Sep.	Oct.	Nov.	Dec.
in.	55.6	5.1	5.2	6.5	5.4	4.4	3.8	5.3	3.7	3.5	2.9	4.4	5.6

Average Snowfall (Years on Record: 48)

	YEAR	Jan.	Feb.	Mar.	Apr.	May	Jun.	Jul.	Aug.	Sep.	Oct.	Nov.	Dec.
in.	1.4	0.5	0.2	0.2	0.1	---	---	---	---	---	---	---	0.4

Average Number of Clear Days (Years on Record: 48)

	YEAR	Jan.	Feb.	Mar.	Apr.	May	Jun.	Jul.	Aug.	Sep.	Oct.	Nov.	Dec.
Days	108	7	7	9	9	8	8	6	9	10	14	10	9

Average Number of Rainy Days (Years on Record: 48)

	YEAR	Jan.	Feb.	Mar.	Apr.	May	Jun.	Jul.	Aug.	Sep.	Oct.	Nov.	Dec.
Days	106	11	9	10	9	9	8	11	9	8	5	8	10

MOBILE, AL

Average Temperature (Years on Record: 48)

	YEAR	Jan.	Feb.	Mar.	Apr.	May	Jun.	Jul.	Aug.	Sep.	Oct.	Nov.	Dec.
°F	68	51	54	60	68	75	80	82	82	78	69	59	53

Average Precipitation (Years on Record: 48)

	YEAR	Jan.	Feb.	Mar.	Apr.	May	Jun.	Jul.	Aug.	Sep.	Oct.	Nov.	Dec.
in.	66	5	5.2	6.6	5.3	5.6	5.3	7.7	6.8	6	3	4.2	5.4

Average Snowfall (Years on Record: 52)

	YEAR	Jan.	Feb.	Mar.	Apr.	May	Jun.	Jul.	Aug.	Sep.	Oct.	Nov.	Dec.
in.	0.5	0.1	0.2	0.1	---	---	---	---	---	---	---	---	0.1

Average Number of Clear Days (Years on Record: 45)

	YEAR	Jan.	Feb.	Mar.	Apr.	May	Jun.	Jul.	Aug.	Sep.	Oct.	Nov.	Dec.
Days	103	8	8	9	9	9	7	4	6	9	14	11	9

Average Number of Rainy Days (Years on Record: 52)

	YEAR	Jan.	Feb.	Mar.	Apr.	May	Jun.	Jul.	Aug.	Sep.	Oct.	Nov.	Dec.
Days	122	11	10	10	7	9	11	16	14	10	6	8	10

MONTGOMERY, AL

Average Temperature (Years on Record: 49)

	YEAR	Jan.	Feb.	Mar.	Apr.	May	Jun.	Jul.	Aug.	Sep.	Oct.	Nov.	Dec.
°F	65	47	51	57	65	73	79	82	81	77	66	56	49

Average Precipitation (Years on Record: 49)

	YEAR	Jan.	Feb.	Mar.	Apr.	May	Jun.	Jul.	Aug.	Sep.	Oct.	Nov.	Dec.
in.	52.7	4.5	5.1	6.1	4.4	4	4	5.2	3.4	4.3	2.5	4.1	5

MONTGOMERY, AL., CONT.

Average Snowfall   (Years on Record: 49)

	YEAR	Jan.	Feb.	Mar.	Apr.	May	Jun.	Jul.	Aug.	Sep.	Oct.	Nov.	Dec.
in.	0.4	0.2	0.1	0.1	---	---	---	---	---	---	---	---	---

Average Number of Clear Days   (Years on Record: 49)

	YEAR	Jan.	Feb.	Mar.	Apr.	May	Jun.	Jul.	Aug.	Sep.	Oct.	Nov.	Dec.
Days	108	7	8	8	10	9	8	6	8	10	14	11	9

Average Number of Rainy Days   (Years on Record: 49)

	YEAR	Jan.	Feb.	Mar.	Apr.	May	Jun.	Jul.	Aug.	Sep.	Oct.	Nov.	Dec.
Days	108	11	9	10	8	9	9	12	9	8	6	8	10

NASHVILLE, TN

Average Temperature   (Years on Record: 48)

	YEAR	Jan.	Feb.	Mar.	Apr.	May	Jun.	Jul.	Aug.	Sep.	Oct.	Nov.	Dec.
°F	60	38	41	50	60	68	76	80	79	72	61	49	41

Average Precipitation   (Years on Record: 48)

	YEAR	Jan.	Feb.	Mar.	Apr.	May	Jun.	Jul.	Aug.	Sep.	Oct.	Nov.	Dec.
in.	47.6	4.3	4.2	5	4	4.6	3.8	3.8	3.3	3.4	2.7	3.9	4.6

Average Snowfall   (Years on Record: 52)

	YEAR	Jan.	Feb.	Mar.	Apr.	May	Jun.	Jul.	Aug.	Sep.	Oct.	Nov.	Dec.
in.	10.2	3.8	3.1	1.4	---	---	---	---	---	---	---	0.4	1.5

Average Number of Clear Days   (Years on Record: 52)

	YEAR	Jan.	Feb.	Mar.	Apr.	May	Jun.	Jul.	Aug.	Sep.	Oct.	Nov.	Dec.
Days	103	7	7	8	8	8	8	8	10	11	13	9	7

Average Number of Rainy Days   (Years on Record: 52)

	YEAR	Jan.	Feb.	Mar.	Apr.	May	Jun.	Jul.	Aug.	Sep.	Oct.	Nov.	Dec.
Days	119	11	11	12	11	11	9	10	9	8	7	9	11

NEW ORLEANS, LA

Average Temperature   (Years on Record: 48)

	YEAR	Jan.	Feb.	Mar.	Apr.	May	Jun.	Jul.	Aug.	Sep.	Oct.	Nov.	Dec.
°F	69	53	56	62	69	75	81	82	82	79	70	61	55

Average Precipitation   (Years on Record: 48)

	YEAR	Jan.	Feb.	Mar.	Apr.	May	Jun.	Jul.	Aug.	Sep.	Oct.	Nov.	Dec.
in.	61.6	5.1	5.5	5.3	4.8	4.9	5.6	6.6	5.9	5.4	2.8	4.5	5.3

Average Number of Clear Days   (Years on Record: 45)

	YEAR	Jan.	Feb.	Mar.	Apr.	May	Jun.	Jul.	Aug.	Sep.	Oct.	Nov.	Dec.
Days	101	7	8	8	8	9	8	4	7	9	15	10	8

Average Number of Rainy Days		(Years on Record: 45)										
	YEAR	Jan.	Feb.	Mar.	Apr.	May	Jun.	Jul.	Aug.	Sep.	Oct.	Nov.	Dec.
Days	114	10	9	9	7	8	11	14	13	10	6	7	10

PADUCAH, KY

Average Temperature		(Years on Record: 38)										
	YEAR	Jan.	Feb.	Mar.	Apr.	May	Jun.	Jul.	Aug.	Sep.	Oct.	Nov.	Dec.
°F	58	34	38	48	58	67	76	79	77	70	59	48	38

Average Precipitation		(Years on Record: 38)										
	YEAR	Jan.	Feb.	Mar.	Apr.	May	Jun.	Jul.	Aug.	Sep.	Oct.	Nov.	Dec.
in.	47.8	3.8	3.8	4.6	4.8	4.5	3.8	4	3.2	3.7	3.1	4	4.4

Average Snowfall		(Years on Record: 10)										
	YEAR	Jan.	Feb.	Mar.	Apr.	May	Jun.	Jul.	Aug.	Sep.	Oct.	Nov.	Dec.
in.	10.6	2.8	4.7	0.6	---	---	---	---	---	---	0.2	---	2.3

Average Number of Clear Days		(Years on Record: 9)										
	YEAR	Jan.	Feb.	Mar.	Apr.	May	Jun.	Jul.	Aug.	Sep.	Oct.	Nov.	Dec.
Days	102	7	6	7	8	7	7	11	11	11	11	9	7

Average Number of Rainy Days		(Years on Record: 10)										
	YEAR	Jan.	Feb.	Mar.	Apr.	May	Jun.	Jul.	Aug.	Sep.	Oct.	Nov.	Dec.
Days	111	8	10	11	11	11	8	8	7	8	9	10	10

RALEIGH-DURHAM, NC

Average Temperature		(Years on Record: 48)										
	YEAR	Jan.	Feb.	Mar.	Apr.	May	Jun.	Jul.	Aug.	Sep.	Oct.	Nov.	Dec.
°F	60	40	43	50	60	67	75	79	77	71	60	51	43

Average Precipitation		(Years on Record: 48)										
	YEAR	Jan.	Feb.	Mar.	Apr.	May	Jun.	Jul.	Aug.	Sep.	Oct.	Nov.	Dec.
in.	41.8	3.5	3.5	3.7	2.8	3.8	3.6	4.4	4.4	3.1	3	2.9	3.1

Average Snowfall		(Years on Record: 49)										
	YEAR	Jan.	Feb.	Mar.	Apr.	May	Jun.	Jul.	Aug.	Sep.	Oct.	Nov.	Dec.
in.	7	2.2	2.6	1.3	---	---	---	---	---	---	---	0.1	0.8

Average Number of Clear Days		(Years on Record: 45)										
	YEAR	Jan.	Feb.	Mar.	Apr.	May	Jun.	Jul.	Aug.	Sep.	Oct.	Nov.	Dec.
Days	111	9	9	9	10	8	8	7	7	10	13	11	10

Average Number of Rainy Days		(Years on Record: 49)										
	YEAR	Jan.	Feb.	Mar.	Apr.	May	Jun.	Jul.	Aug.	Sep.	Oct.	Nov.	Dec.
Days	112	10	10	10	9	10	9	11	10	8	7	8	9

SAVANNAH, GA

Average Temperature   (Years on Record: 45)

	YEAR	Jan.	Feb.	Mar.	Apr.	May	Jun.	Jul.	Aug.	Sep.	Oct.	Nov.	Dec.
°F	67	49	53	59	66	74	79	82	81	77	68	59	52

Average Precipitation   (Years on Record: 45)

	YEAR	Jan.	Feb.	Mar.	Apr.	May	Jun.	Jul.	Aug.	Sep.	Oct.	Nov.	Dec.
in.	50.3	3.5	3.1	3.9	3.2	4.2	5.6	6.8	7.2	5	2.9	2.2	2.7

SHREVEPORT, LA

Average Temperature   (Years on Record: 48)

	YEAR	Jan.	Feb.	Mar.	Apr.	May	Jun.	Jul.	Aug.	Sep.	Oct.	Nov.	Dec.
°F	66	46	50	58	66	73	80	83	83	77	67	56	49

Average Precipitation   (Years on Record: 48)

	YEAR	Jan.	Feb.	Mar.	Apr.	May	Jun.	Jul.	Aug.	Sep.	Oct.	Nov.	Dec.
in.	46.9	4.1	4	3.7	4.6	5.1	4.1	3.6	2.5	3.1	3.7	4.1	4.2

Average Snowfall   (Years on Record: 41)

	YEAR	Jan.	Feb.	Mar.	Apr.	May	Jun.	Jul.	Aug.	Sep.	Oct.	Nov.	Dec.
in.	1.7	0.8	0.5	0.2	---	---	---	---	---	---	---	---	0.2

Average Number of Clear Days   (Years on Record: 41)

	YEAR	Jan.	Feb.	Mar.	Apr.	May	Jun.	Jul.	Aug.	Sep.	Oct.	Nov.	Dec.
Days	114	8	8	9	8	8	8	10	11	11	13	11	9

Average Number of Rainy Days   (Years on Record: 41)

	YEAR	Jan.	Feb.	Mar.	Apr.	May	Jun.	Jul.	Aug.	Sep.	Oct.	Nov.	Dec.
Days	98	10	8	9	9	9	8	8	7	7	7	8	9

TUPELO, MS

Average Temperature   (Years on Record: 13)

	YEAR	Jan.	Feb.	Mar.	Apr.	May	Jun.	Jul.	Aug.	Sep.	Oct.	Nov.	Dec.
°F	63	41	46	54	62	70	78	81	80	74	63	53	44

Average Precipitation   (Years on Record: 13)

	YEAR	Jan.	Feb.	Mar.	Apr.	May	Jun.	Jul.	Aug.	Sep.	Oct.	Nov.	Dec.
in.	51.9	3.4	5.7	4.8	4.1	5.6	4.7	2.8	3	3	3.7	5	6.2

Average Snowfall   (Years on Record: 10)

	YEAR	Jan.	Feb.	Mar.	Apr.	May	Jun.	Jul.	Aug.	Sep.	Oct.	Nov.	Dec.
in.	2.9	1.4	0.8	0.3	---	---	---	---	---	---	---	---	0.

Average Number of Clear Days   (Years on Record: 10)

	YEAR	Jan.	Feb.	Mar.	Apr.	May	Jun.	Jul.	Aug.	Sep.	Oct.	Nov.	Dec.
Days	119	8	7	8	10	8	10	11	11	13	14	9	8

Average Number of Rainy Days   (Years on Record: 10)

	YEAR	Jan.	Feb.	Mar.	Apr.	May	Jun.	Jul.	Aug.	Sep.	Oct.	Nov.	Dec.
Days	109	10	10	10	9	12	10	8	8	7	8	8	11

Red Sky at Night...

Country folk have been forecasting the weather for centuries, looking at the skies and behavior of plants, animals, and even their own bodies for clues to future weather patterns. Satellites, radar, and sophisticated equipment provide more accurate predictions today, but many of the old weather indicators still hold true. Test them for yourself and draw your own conclusions!

"Red sky at night, sailor's delight. Red sky in the morning, sailors take warning."
In a clear western sky, red sunsets occur when the light shines through dust particles. If a sky is red in the eastern morning sky, it indicates a high pressure has already passed through, meaning a low pressure bringing bad weather will soon follow.

Cricket chirps indicate air temperature. Count the number of cricket chirps in 15 seconds and add 40; the total will usually be within one degree of the air temperature.

"If a cat washes her face o'er her ear, 'tis a sign weather will be fine and clear."
When dry weather increases static electricity, cats groom more to wet their fur.

The presence of lots of woolly worms with dark, thick hair predicts a hard winter.

"Halo around the sun or moon, rain or snow soon."
The halo is a layer of cirrus clouds made of ice crystals, which act like a light prism. These clouds often precede an approaching warm front with a low pressure system, bringing bad weather. If the circle is large, it will rain soon. Several concentric circles mean a long period of wet weather.

If berries or nuts are plentiful and squirrels bury them early, it will be a hard winter.

A drop in barometric pressure, which precedes bad weather or thunderstorms, often causes aches and pains in people with joint diseases, bad teeth, or bunions. Sensing the change in pressure, many dogs become very agitated long before a thunderstorm arrives.

"Trout jump high when a rain is nigh."
As air pressure drops, trapped gases in decaying plants in the bottoms of ponds and lakes is released, dispersing the microorganisms hiding in the debris. Fish often jump out of the water in the feeding frenzy that ensues.

"Clear moon, frost soon."
If the temperature is low enough on clear, winter nights, frost may form by morning.

The morning glory opens its petals in sunny weather and closes them when rain is expected.

The first twelve days of the year are thought to foretell the weather for each of the next twelve months.

"When the dew is on the grass, rain will never come to pass. When grass is dry at morning light, look for rain before the night."

"If the rooster crows on going to bed, you may rise with a watery head."
A decrease in atmospheric pressure causes creatures to be restless.

"Fish bite least with wind in the east."
Easterly winds indicate bad weather, when fish tend to be less active near the surface of the water.

"If birds fly low, expect rain and a blow."
In bad weather, when the air pressure is low and less dense, birds cannot fly as high.

"When the swallow's nest is high, summer is dry. When the swallow's nest is low, you can safely reap and sow."
Large numbers of birds sitting on telephone wires foretells rain.

The last Sunday in the month indicates the weather of the next month.

"A cow with its tail to the west makes the weather best, a cow with its tail to the east makes the weather least."
Cows also lay down in a field when rain is coming, sensing the moisture in the air and wanting a dry spot to lay.

"If the oak flowers before the ash, then we are in for a splash. But if the ash flowers before the oak, we are in for a soak."
Expect either light rain, or a period of wet weather.

LIGHTNING: A SHOCKING STORY

We've all seen it. But what *is* it, exactly? Simply put, lightning is an electrostatic discharge produced during a thunderstorm between negatively charged clouds and positive charges on the ground (including the ground itself, buildings, flagpoles, boat masts, trees, mountains, and yes—people). Normally the ground has a negative charge with respect to the atmosphere, but the strong negative charge at the bottom of the cloud produces positive charges below it. This discharge heads *downward,* and when it gets within 150 feet of a positive charge the two make a channel, and electricity from the ground surges *upward* causing a flash. Air is a poor conductor of electricity, so by the time a charge builds up, it's massive. In these few split-seconds of current, electricity superheats the surrounding air to a temperature five times hotter than the surface of the sun! And what of thunder? The air around the channel expands rapidly in the heat, producing vibrations—shockwaves—that we hear as thunder.

If you're caught on a golf course during a storm and are afraid, just hold up a 1-iron. Not even God can hit a 1-iron.

—LEE TREVINO

STRUCK BY LIGHTNING?

This is one club we don't want to join, but if you should be struck by lightning (and, well, survive), you can join the Lightning Strike and Electric Shock Survivors International Inc. (LSESSI), a nonprofit support group. With its motto, "Join us if it strikes you," and newsletter, *Hit or Miss,* the group emphasizes the necessity of a sense of humor in overcoming trauma.

TYPES OF LIGHTNING

Intracloud lightning (anvil crawlers): Lights up the cloud from the inside out.

Cloud-to-ground lightning: Second most common type, after intracloud.

Bead lightning, ribbon lightning: Cloud-to-ground that is extra luminous, leaving a momentary trail of beads or ribbons.

Cloud-to-cloud lighting: Pretty rare

Ground-to-cloud lightning Most often occurring in summer.

Heat lightning: Just faint flashes of lightning at a great distance.

Ball lightning: Rarely recorded on film, a floating ball of electricity, sometimes dissipates with a bang.

LIGHTNING SAFETY

WARNINGS
- Distant thunder or lightning is an important warning.
- Hair standing on end; skin prickling.

DO
- Check the weather forecast before hiking.
- When out of doors, watch for thunder clouds and listen for distant thunder.
- Take shelter immediately; a building is safest, or a car with the windows rolled up.
- Avoid open spaces, fields, ballparks, golf courses.
- If you're boating, get off the water.
- If caught outside during a thunderstorm, get as low as possible.
- Indoors, stay away from metal items (stove, refrigerator, water faucets) and windows.

DON'T
- Stand under a tree.
- Take a shower during a thunderstorm.
- Use the phone.

It's Not the Heat, It's the Humidity!

We know hot in the South. And humid. And miserable. Yes, we know we tell people, "It's not the heat, it's the humidity" and we mean it when we say it. Even our relatively mild temperatures can feel miserably hot because of our high levels of humidity. Humidity is the amount of water vapor in the air, usually measured relative to the air's moisture-holding capacity. So, at 100% humidity (at the current temperature), the air is at its saturation point and it's probably raining (if you're lucky). But somehow, knowing *why* something is happening doesn't really make it any better. Sometimes all you can do is laugh. So, how hot is it?

... It's so hot, the birds are using oven mitts to pull worms out of the ground.

... It's so hot, the cows are giving evaporated milk.

... It's so hot, the trees are whistling for the dogs.

... It's so hot, potatoes can cook underground; all you have to do is pull them out, and butter and salt them.

... It's so hot, farmers are feeding ice to the hens to prevent them from laying hard-boiled eggs.

... It's so hot, dogs are still chasing cats, but they are both walking.

... It's so hot, you discover how few fingers it takes to turn the steering wheel.

... It's so hot, the apple trees are making apple crisp.

... It's so hot, you realize asphalt can also be a liquid.

... It's so hot, the ceiling fans are asking for a raise.

It's not the heat, it's the humility.

—YOGI BERRA

HEAT SAFETY TIPS

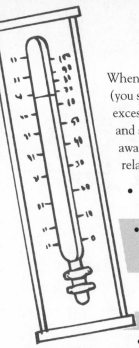

When it's 95° all bodily heat loss occurs through evaporation (you sweat, it dries and wicks away the heat). But when it's also excessively humid (say, over 75 percent), evaporation slows and sweating becomes very inefficient—so it's important to be aware of heat conditions and take precautions to avoid heat-related illnesses.

- Make sure you are hydrated by drinking lots of fluids before, during, and after heat exposure.
- Sports drinks are better than water for fluid replacement; carbonated drinks, caffeine, and alcohol are counterproductive.
- Wear lightweight, porous, loose-fitting clothing to promote heat loss.
- Wear light-colored clothing.
- If clothes become sweaty, change them.
- Certain antibiotics cause susceptibility to heat illness; watch for symptoms.
- Acclimate to heat conditions gradually. Take regular breaks.
- Avoid taking salt tablets unless advised to do so by a physician.

HEAT ILLNESS SYMPTOMS

1. **Heat cramps:** painful muscle spasms. Drink fluids.

2. **Heat exhaustion:** profuse sweating, flushed skin, elevated temperature, dizziness, hyperventilation, nausea, headache, and rapid pulse. Treat immediately by drinking large quantities of water. Remove wet clothing to facilitate evaporation.

3. **Heat stroke:** sudden collapse and loss of consciousness, pale skin, may or may not be sweating, hot dry skin, vomiting, shallow breathing, and a temperature of 106 degrees or higher. Can occur suddenly and without warning. Call 911. Remove clothing and put into a cool (not cold) bath, or wrap in wet sheets and begin fanning.

WORST CITIES IN THE U.S. FOR ALLERGIES

1. Hartford, CT
2. Greenville, SC
3. Boston, MA
4. Detroit, MI
5. Orlando, FL
6. Knoxville, TN
7. Omaha, NE
8. Sacramento, CA
9. Washington, DC
10. Baltimore, MD
11. New York, NY
12. Louisville, KY
13. Rochester, NY
14. Houston, TX
15. New Orleans, LA

Source: Forbes.com / Asthma and Allergy Foundation of America

Whatever Floats Your Cardboard Boat

Southerners love a race—any kind of race. But a *cardboard boat race??* Now that's different. How in heck do you keep a cardboard boat from sinking? Held every July since 1987, in Heber Springs, Arkansas (near Little Rock), the cardboard boat regatta has become a festival that draws ambitious boat builders and racers from all over the United States. Many teams return yearly, spending their winters coming up with designs that will take the coveted award. Imagine over one hundred outrageous boats, with crews of one to eight, paddling the 200-yard course as they jockey for first position—so long as they don't sink first!

Basically, boats must be fashioned from cardboard, duct tape, glue and paint—no epoxy or fiberglass allowed. Creativity rules, and some builders turn cardboard poster tubes into pontoons. While paddles are the traditional form of propulsion, many eager designers have turned to human-powered paddlewheels in their need for speed.

Cardboard boats may be as small as a bathtub, or as large as a pirate ship. The only limitation is ingenuity. The annual championship receives national media coverage every year. The festival ends with a Cardboard Boat Demolition Derby and fireworks display.

THE MOST EXCITING TWO MINUTES IN SPORTS

Run on the one and one-quarter mile track at Churchill Downs in Louisville, Kentucky, the fabled Kentucky Derby is a stakes race for three-year-old thoroughbred horses, and is the first leg of the Triple Crown (the other races are the Preakness Stakes at Pimlico Race Course in Baltimore, Maryland, and the Belmont Stakes at Belmont Park in Elmont, New York).

But the Derby is special. The main event of the three-week long Derby Festival, the race is run each year on the first Saturday in May. "My Old Kentucky Home" is the theme song as the horses parade pre-race, elegant women wear large hats, and copious amounts of mint juleps are consumed. The governor of Kentucky awards the winner a trophy and a blanket of red roses, earning the race its nickname, "The Run for the Roses."

MINT JULEP

4 sprigs fresh mint
2 ½ oz. bourbon
1 tsp. sugar
2 tsp. water

Crush mint leaves and sugar in a Tom Collins glass. Fill with cracked ice and bourbon. Stir until glass frosts. Serve with straw and garnish with mint sprig. 1 serving.

The Most Controversial Decision in Triple Crown Racing

In 1968, Forward Pass won the Derby via disqualification. The favorite in all three races, Forward Pass lost to Dancer's Image by 1½ lengths in the Derby—but Dancer's Image was later disqualified when phenylbutazone was found in his post-race urine sample. Although the drug was legal at some racetracks, Churchill Downs was not among them at that time.

KENTUCKY DERBY WINNERS

YEAR	NAME	YEAR	NAME
1875	Aristides	1904	Elwood
1876	Vagrant	1905	Agile
1877	Baden Baden	1906	Sir Huon
1878	Day Star	1907	Pink Star
1879	Lord Murphy	1908	Stone Street
1880	Fonso	1909	Wintergreen
1881	Hindoo	1910	Donau
1882	Apollo	1911	Meridian
1883	Leonatus	1912	Worth
1884	Buchanan	1913	Donerail
1885	Joe Cotton	1914	Old Rosebud
1886	Ben Ali	1915	Regret
1887	Montrose	1916	George Smith
1888	Macbeth II	1917	Omar Khayyam
1889	Spokane	1918	Exterminator
1890	Riley	1919	Sir Barton †
1891	Kingman	1920	Paul Jones
1892	Azra	1921	Behave Yourself
1893	Lookout	1922	Morvich
1894	Chant	1923	Zev
1895	Halma	1924	Black Gold
1896	Ben Brush	1925	Flying Ebony
1897	Typhoon II	1926	Bubbling Over
1898	Plaudit	1927	Whiskery
1899	Manuel	1928	Reigh Count
1900	Lieut. Gibson	1929	Clyde Van Dusen
1901	His Eminence	1930	Gallant Fox †
1902	Alan-a-Dale	1931	Twenty Grand
1903	Judge Himes	1932	Burgoo King

1933	Brokers Tip	1971	Canonero II
1934	Cavalcade	1972	Riva Ridge
1935	Omaha †	1973	Secretariat †
1936	Bold Venture	1974	Cannonade
1937	War Admiral †	1975	Foolish Pleasure
1938	Lawrin	1976	Bold Forbes
1939	Johnstown	1977	Seattle Slew †
1940	Gallahadion	1978	Affirmed †
1941	Whirlaway †	1979	Spectacular Bid
1942	Shut Out	1980	Genuine Risk
1943	Count Fleet †	1981	Pleasant Colony
1944	Pensive	1982	Gato Del Sol
1945	Hoop Jr.	1983	Sunny's Halo
1946	Assault †	1984	Swale
1947	Jet Pilot	1985	Spend a Buck
1948	Citation †	1986	Ferdinand
1949	Ponder	1987	Alysheba
1950	Middleground	1988	Winning Colors
1951	Count Turf	1989	Sunday Silence
1952	Hill Gail	1990	Unbridled
1953	Dark Star	1991	Strike the Gold
1954	Determine	1992	Lil E. Tee
1955	Swaps	1993	Sea Hero
1956	Needles	1994	Go for Gin
1957	Iron Liege	1995	Thunder Gulch
1958	Tim Tam	1996	Grindstone
1959	Tomy Lee	1997	Silver Charm
1960	Venetian Way	1998	Real Quiet
1961	Carry Back	1999	Charismatic
1962	Decidedly	2000	Fusaichi Pegasus
1963	Chateaugay	2001	Monarchos
1964	Northern Dancer	2002	War Emblem
1965	Lucky Debonair	2003	Funny Cide
1966	Kauai King	2004	Smarty Jones
1967	Proud Clarion	2005	Giacomo
1968	Forward Pass*	2006	Barbaro
1969	Majestic Prince		
1970	Dust Commander		

A † designates a Triple Crown Winner.

THAT DOG WON'T HUNT!

A popular sport in the South—where the love of dogs, horses, and hunting goes hand-in-hand—is field trials. For the uninitiated, field trials is a competitive event during which a hunting dog's ability to perform in the field—whether pointing and retrieving a downed bird or trailing a rabbit—is judged. Basically, can my dog beat your dog? (Heck, yeah!)

Field trials are a big social event. The dog handlers and judges often ride alongside on horseback (usually "easy going" breeds such as Tennessee Walking horses). Whether riding or walking, the dog handlers, judges, officials and spectators follow the dogs along designated courses. Dogs are paired two to a brace and several braces run each day. When a dog points, the judges verify the point, the handler dismounts and walks over to the dog, flushes out the bird and shoots blanks into the air.

Bird dogs (pointers and setters) and retrievers are the most popular breeds in the South for field trials, where hunting is a way of life. The pointing breed field trial dogs work from carefully bred inherited instincts and training. They are rated on their ability to aid the hunter find game birds, flush them for the shot, then retrieve each bird in good condition.

The most common retrieving breeds are the golden, the Labrador, and the American Chesapeake retrievers. Trials are a little different for retrieving breeds, due to their inherent abilities. In a marked retrieve, the dog sees the bird fall and is judged on his ability to find and retrieve the bird quickly. In a blind retrieve, where terrain hides the fallen bird, the dog depends on the handler to direct him. In the popular retriever hunting tests, the dog is rated on alertness, eagerness, and speed in retrieving a bird from land or water.

Hundreds of clubs sponsor licensed field trials for individual dogs and packs. Serious hunters enjoy taking their dogs to the trials to keep their skills sharpened and their dogs in top performance. West Tennessee has a rich sporting dog heritage due to its close proximity to the Mississippi flyway, which attracts waterfowl hunters. Recognized as the birthplace of pointing dog field trials, Grand Junction, Tennessee also boasts the Field Trial Hall of Fame, National Bird Dog Museum, and National Retriever Museum. Union Springs, Alabama calls itself the "Bird Dog Field Trial Capital of the World" and displays a full-sized monument of an English pointer in tribute to the sport and the men and dogs who participate. The National Amateur Free-for-All is held in February each year.

"That dog just ain't gonna hunt" is a saying you'll hear in the South, but it doesn't have anything to do with hunting dogs. It's usually said to describe a plan or scheme that will fail, or does not fulfill its intended purpose.

WE GOT YOUR BASE BALL

CLASS	TEAM	LEAGUE	AFFILIATE
Alabama			
AA	Huntsville Stars	Southern	Milwaukee Brewers
AA	Birmingham Barons	Southern	Chicago White Sox
AA	Montgomery Biscuits	Southern	Tampa Bay Devil Rays
AA	Mobile BayBears	Southern	San Diego Padres
Georgia			
PRO	Atlanta Braves	National	n/a
Kentucky			
AAA	Louisville Bats	International	Cincinnati Reds
Louisiana			
AAA	New Orleans Zephyrs	Pacific Coast	Washington Nationals
Mississippi			
AA	Mississippi Braves (Jackson)	Southern	Atlanta Braves
North Carolina			
AA	Carolina Mudcats (Raleigh)	Southern	Florida Marlins
AAA	Charlotte Knights	International	Chicago White Sox
AAA	Durham Bulls	International	Tampa Bay Devil Rays
Tennessee			
AA	Chattanooga Lookouts	Southern	Cincinnati Reds
AAA	Memphis Redbirds	Pacific Coast	St. Louis Cardinals
AAA	Nashville Sounds	Pacific Coast	Milwaukee Brewers
AA	Tennessee Smokies (Knoxville)	Southern	Arizona Diamondbacks
AA	West TN Diamond Jazz (Jackson)	Southern	Chicago Cubs
Virginia			
AAA	Norfolk Tides	International	New York Mets
AAA	Richmond Braves	International	Atlanta Braves

SOUTHERNERS IN THE BASEBALL HALL OF FAME

NAME	BIRTHPLACE	YEAR INDUCTED
Hank Aaron	Mobile, AL	1982
Luke Appling	High Point, NC	1964
Cool Papa Bell	Starckville, MS	1974
George Brett	Glen Dale, WV	1999
Lou Brock	El Dorado, AR	1985
Jim Bunning	Southgate, KY	1996
Jesse Burckett	Wheeling, WV	1946
Happy Chandler	Corydon, KY	1982
Ty Cobb	Narrows, GA	1936
Earle Combs	Pebworth, KY	1970
Ray Dandridge	Richmond, VA	1987
Leon Day	Alexandria, VA	1995
Dizzy Dean	Lucas, AR	1953
Bill Dickey	Bastrop, LA	1954
Larry Doby	Camden, SC	1998
Rick Ferrell	Durham, NC	1984
Bill Foster	Rodney, MS	1996
Josh Gibson	Buena Vista, GA	1972
Catfish Hunter	Hertford, NC	1987
Monte Irvin	Columbia, AL	1973
Travis Jackson	Waldo, AR	1982
George Kell	Swifton, AR	1983
Buck Leonard	Rocky Mount, NC	1972
Ted Lyons	Lake Charles, LA	1955
Lee MacPhail	Nashville, TN	1998
Heinie Manush	Tuscumbia, AL	1964
Willie Mayes	Westfield, AL	1971
Bill Mazeroski	Wheeling, WV	2001
Willie McCovey	Mobile, AL	1986
Johnny Mize	Demorest, GA	1982
Mel Ott	Gretna, LA	1951
Satchel Paige	Mobile, AL	1971
Gaylord Perry	Williamston, NC	1991
Eppa Rixey	Culpeper, VA	1963
Brooks Robinson	Little Rock, AR	1983
Jackie Robinson	Cairo, GA	1962
Joe Sewell	Titus, AL	1977
Enos Slaughter	Roxboro, NC	1985
Ozzie Smith	Mobile, AL	2002
Turkey Stearnes	Nashville, TN	2000
Don Sutton	Clio, AL	1998
Bill Terry	Atlanta, GA	1954
Joseph "Arky" Vaughan	Clifty, AR	1985
Hoyt Wilhelm	Huntersville, NC	1985
Billy Williams	Whistler, AL	1987
Early Wynn	Hartford, AL	1972

Hunstville Stars

Named for the nearby NASA operations, former Stars include Mark McGwire, Jose Canseco, Stan Javier, Tim Hudson, Miguel Tejada, Ken Caminiti, and Jason Giambi.

Carolina Mudcats

When you pay your admission fee to see the Mudcats play, you don't get a ticket—you get a fishing license.

HAMMERIN' HANK

Born and raised in Mobile, Alabama, Henry Aaron was such a talented baseball player that before he turned fifteen he was playing on a semi-pro team. Although his mother wanted him to go to college, he left high school to play for the Indianapolis Clowns of the Negro American League in 1951, and by 1952 he'd been signed by the Braves (then in Boston, later in Milwaukee before moving to Atlanta in 1965). Aaron was the last Negro League player to make the jump to the major leagues before it was disbanded. After a series of spectacular years, by 1969 Aaron had moved into third place on the career home run list, moving past Mickey Mantle and behind Willie Mays and Babe Ruth. By 1973 the race to beat the Babe had heated up, and so had racism: Aaron received thousands of threats and hate-filled mail. A humble man, Aaron has said that he was "changed" by the volume and depth of hatred … although it did no good: in 1974, on the home field in Atlanta, Hank Aaron broke Babe Ruth's all-time home run record, hitting his 732nd homer. After being traded o the Milwaukee Brewers, Aaron broke baseball's all time RBI record on May 1, 1975, and on July 20, 1976, Hank Aaron hit his 755th—and final—home run. His jersey, number 44, has been retired by both the Atlanta Braves and the Milwaukee Brewers. Both teams display statues of Aaron outside their ballparks (and the address of Turner Field is 755 Hank Aaron Drive SE, in honor of his 755 career home runs). Henry Aaron has come closer than any other player to achieving baseball's "triple crown"—first in all-time homers, first in all-time RBIs, third in all-time hits—and at the time of his retirement he was first in all-time games played and all-time at-bats. He is the all-time total bases leader and extra-base hits leader, won three Golden Glove awards, and has been awarded the Presidential Medal of Freedom (2002), the nation's highest civilian honor.

The pitcher has got only a ball. I've got a bat.
So the percentage in weapons is in my favor
and I let the fellow with the ball do the fretting.

—HENRY "HANK" AARON

The Sport of Southern Politics

Well, okay, if you're going to get all technical about it, poking fun at the government isn't really a sport. Or is it? Here are just a few of the funny laws in the South:

Alabama – It's illegal to wear a fake moustache that causes laughter in church.

Arkansas – In Little Rock, if a man and woman flirt with each other in the streets, they can be jailed for 30 days.

Georgia – There is a law prohibiting one to say, "oh boy" in public in Jonesborough.

Kentucky – It's illegal to remarry the same man four times.

Louisiana – It's against the law to gargle in public.

Mississippi – It's against the law to kill a squirrel with a shotgun in a courtroom.

North Carolina – You cannot use elephants to plow cotton fields.

South Carolina – No horses are allowed in the Fountain Inn unless they're wearing pants.

Tennessee – It's illegal to shoot any game from automobiles, other than whales.

Virginia – It's illegal to flip a coin in a restaurant to determine who is going to pay for the coffee.

West Virginia – No clergy may tell jokes or funny stories from the pulpit in Nicholas County.

THE GREATEST GOLFER WHO EVER LIVED

Born into a wealthy family in Atlanta, Georgia, Robert Tyre "Bobby" Jones was a child golf prodigy who became one of the greatest golfers who ever lived.

Sickly as a young boy and unable to eat solid food until he was five years old, his health improved when the family moved next to the fairways of Atlanta's East Lake Country Club. At six, Jones was swinging a cut-down one iron given to him by a neighbor, and at seven he was mimicking the swing of the country club pro. At 11 he shot an 80 on the course at East Lake, and at 12 Bobby Jones shot 70 and won two club championships.

He played in his first U.S Amateur championship at the age of 14, but for the next seven years struggled with his temper and many club-throwing incidents.

> *The secret of golf is to turn three shots into two.*
>
> —**BOBBY JONES**

Jones finally conquered his temper, and at 21 won his first U.S. Open at Inwood Country Club in New York. From 1923 to 1929, Jones played in 21 national championships and won 13 of them. Now an even-tempered Georgia gentleman, he swung his way into the nation's heart by his supreme sportsmanship. Perhaps the most distinguished shot of his career was in that first U.S. Open title game when, with his two iron, he drilled the ball from the edge of the rough, over water, to within eight feet of the pin. Two putts later he had won his first major, and launched on a seven-year winning streak that culminated in winning what became known as the Grand Slam in 1930. At that time, the Grand Slam

meant winning the U.S. Open, U.S. Amateur, British Open, and British Amateur, all in the same year. It remains one of the greatest sports achievements of all time.

Jones retired from professional golf at 28, by then also a graduate of Georgia Tech and Harvard, and a practicing lawyer. He founded the Augusta National Golf Club and the Masters, and would emerge from his retirement once a year to play in the Masters. He helped design the first-ever matched set of golf clubs (including identifying clubs by number, rather than by name), and produced instructional golf videos and movie shorts. Perhaps his most enduring legacy in addition to his example of sportsmanship is his design for the Augusta National, still considered one of the world's finest courses.

In 1948, Jones was diagnosed with syringomyelia, a rare disease of the central nervous system, and never played golf again. Confined to a wheelchair, he would still host the Masters until his death in 1971 at 69. Golfers at St. Andrews in Scotland stopped play as the clubhouse flag was lowered in tribute. He was among the first to be inducted into the World Golf Hall of Fame in 1974.

Bobby Jones demonstrates the swing that made him a champion.

Jones, who possessed a supremely graceful swing, never let what could be considered this ultimate irony get him down. "We all have to play the ball as it lies," he said. He is remembered for the incredible legacy he left for the greatest game ever played.

THE BASKETBALL HALL OF FAME

To be considered for induction, a player must be retired from play for at least five years, while a coach or referee must be retired for at least five years or have been active full-time on the professional, collegiate, or high school level for at least twenty-five years. Contributors must simply have made a "significant contribution to the game of basketball."

NAME	BIRTHPLACE	POSITION
Charles Wade Barkley	Leeds, AL	Player
Leon Barmore	Ruston, LA	Coach
Walter Jones Belamy	New Bern, NC	Player
David Williams Cowans	Newport, KY	Player
Joan Crawford	Fort Smith, AR	Player
Edgar A. Diddle	Gradyville, KY	Coach
Clyde Austin "The Glide" Drexler	New Orleans, LA	Player
Joe Dumars	Shreveport, LA	Player
Alex English	Columbia, SC	Player
Harry Fisher	Gradyville, KY	Contributor
Walter "Clyde" Frazier	Atlanta, GA	Player
Joseph Franklin "Jumping Joe" Fulks	Birmingham, KY	Player
Clarence E. "Big House" Gaines	Paducah, KY	Coach
William "Pop" Gates	Decatur, AL	Player
Harold Everett Greer	Huntington, WV	Player
Sue Gunter	Baton Rouge, LA	Coach
Clifford Oldham Hagan	Owensboro, KY	Player
Elvin Ernest Hayes	Rayville, LA	Player
Bailey E. Howell	Middleton, TN	Player
Samuel "Sam" Jones	Wilmington, NC	Player
George "Meadowlark" Lemon	Wilmington, NC	Contributor
Earl Francis Lloyd	Alexandria, Virginia	Contributor
Moses E. Malone	Petersburg, VA	Player
Robert Allen "Bob" McAdoo	Greensboro, NC	Player
Charles Martin "C.M." Newton	Rockwood, TN	Contributor
Robert Lee Parish	Shreveport, LA	Player
Robert E. Lee "Bob" Pettit	Baton Rouge, LA	Player
Frank Vernon Ramsey Jr.	Corydon, KY	Player
Willis Reed Jr.	Bernice, LA	Player
Arnold D. Risen	Williamstown, KY	Player
Oscar Palmer Robertson	Charlotte, TN	Player

NAME	BIRTHPLACE	POSITION
William Felton Russell	Monroe, LA	Player
Pat Summitt Head	Henrietta, TN	Coach
David O'Neil Thompson	Shelby, NC	Player
Westley Sissel "Wes" Unseld	Louisville, KY	Player
L. Margaret Wade	McCool, MS	Coach
Jerome Alan West	Chelyan, WV	Player
Nera White	Lafayette, TN	Player
Morgan Wootten	Durham, NC	Coach
Phil Woolpert	Danville, KY	Coach
James Ager Worthy	Gastonia, NC	Player
Sandra Kay Yow	Gibsonville, NC	Coach

NCAA TOURNAMENT APPEARANCES

# TIMES	SCHOOL
46	Kentucky
37	North Carolina
36	UCLA
34	Kansas
32	Indiana
31	Louisville

NCAA TOURNAMENT VICTORIES

# TIMES	SCHOOL
96	Kentucky
88	North Carolina
83	Duke
80	UCLA
73	Kansas
58	Indiana

TOP 5 NCAA CHAMPIONSHIP WINNERS

# TIMES	SCHOOL	YEARS
11	UCLA	'95, '75, '67–'73, 64–'65
7	Kentucky	'98, '96, '78, '58, 51, '4–'49
5	Indiana	'87, '81, '76, '53, '40
4	N. Carolina	'05, '93, '82, '57
3	Duke	'01, '91–'92

SEC Football Schedule

It never hurts to plan ahead, sometimes *way* ahead. Here are the SEC Football schedules. Only death and taxes are certain, so visit **www.secsports.com** for the latest details and any schedule updates.

DATE	OPPONENT	DATE	OPPONENT
ALABAMA		Nov. 4	Arkansas State
Sept. 2	Hawaii	Nov. 11	Georgia
Sept. 9	Vanderbilt	Nov. 18	at Alabama
Sept. 16	Louisiana-Monroe	**FLORIDA**	
Sept. 23	at Arkansas	Sept. 2	Southern Miss
Sept. 30	at Florida	Sept. 9	Central Florida
Oct. 7	Duke	Sept. 16	at Tennessee
Oct. 14	Ole Miss	Sept. 23	Kentucky
Oct. 28	Florida International	Sept. 30	Alabama
		Oct. 7	LSU
Nov. 4	Mississippi State	Oct. 14	at Auburn
Nov. 11	at LSU	Oct. 28	vs. Georgia (Jacksonville)
Nov. 18	Auburn		
ARKANSAS		Nov. 4	Vanderbilt
Sept. 2	Southern California	Nov. 11	South Carolina
Sept. 9	Utah State	Nov. 18	Western Carolina
Sept. 16	at Vanderbilt	Nov. 25	at Florida State
Sept. 23	Alabama	**GEORGIA**	
Oct. 7	at Auburn	Sept. 2	Western Kentucky
Oct. 14	Southeast Missouri St.	Sept. 9	at South Carolina
Oct. 21	Ole Miss	Sept. 16	UAB
Oct. 28	Louisiana-Monroe (at Little Rock)	Sept. 23	Colorado
		Sept. 30	at Ole Miss
Nov. 4	at South Carolina	Oct. 7	Tennessee
Nov. 11	Tennessee	Oct. 21	Mississippi State
Nov. 18	at Mississippi State	Oct. 28	vs. Florida (Jacksonville)
Nov. 25	LSU (at Little Rock)		
AUBURN		Nov. 4	at Kentucky
Sept. 2	Washington State	Nov. 11	at Auburn
Sept. 9	at Mississippi State	Nov. 25	Georgia Tech
Sept. 16	LSU	**KENTUCKY**	
Sept. 23	Buffalo	Sept. 2	at Louisville
Sept. 28	at South Carolina	Sept. 9	Texas State
Oct. 7	Arkansas	Sept. 16	Ole Miss
Oct. 14	Florida	Sept. 23	at Florida
Oct. 21	Tulane	Sept. 30	Central Michigan
Oct. 28	at Ole Miss		

I DIDN'T KNOW THAT ALMANAC SOUTHERN EDITION 2007

DATE	OPPONENT	DATE	OPPONENT
Oct. 7	South Carolina	Nov. 4	at Alabama
Oct. 14	at LSU	Nov. 18	Arkansas
Oct. 28	at MississippiState	Nov. 25	at Ole Miss
Nov. 4	Georgia		
Nov. 11	Vanderbilt	**SOUTH CAROLINA**	
Nov. 18	Louisiana-Monroe	Aug. 31	at Mississippi State
Nov. 25	at Tennessee LSU	Sept. 9	Georgia
Sept. 2	Louisiana-Lafaette	Sept. 16	Wofford
Sept. 9	Arizona	Sept. 23	Florida Atlantic
Sept. 16	at Auburn	Sept. 28	Auburn
Sept. 23	Tulane	Oct. 7	at Kentucky
Sept. 30	Mississippi State	Oct. 21	at Vanderbilt
Oct. 7	at Florida	Oct. 28	Tennessee
Oct. 14	Kentucky	Nov. 4	Arkansas
Oct. 21	Fresno State	Nov. 11	at Florida
Nov. 4	at Tennessee	Nov. 18	Middle Tennessee
Nov. 11	Alabama	Nov. 25	at Clemson
Nov. 18	Ole Miss		
Nov. 25	at Arkansas	**TENNESSEE**	
	(Little Rock)	Sept. 2	California
OLE MISS		Sept. 9	Air Force
Sept. 2	Memphis	Sept. 16	Florida
Sept. 9	at Missouri	Sept. 23	Marshall
Sept. 16	at Kentucky	Sept. 30	at Memphis
Sept. 23	Wake Forest	Oct. 7	at Georgia
Sept. 30	Georgia	Oct. 21	Alabama
Oct. 7	Vanderbilt	Oct. 28	at South Carolina
Oct. 14	at Alabama	Nov. 4	LSU
Oct. 21	at Arkansas	Nov. 11	at Arkansas
Oct. 28	Auburn	Nov. 18	at Vanderbilt
Nov. 4	Northwestern State	Nov. 25	Kentucky
Nov. 18	at LSU		
Nov. 25	Mississippi State	**VANDERBILT**	
		Sept. 2	at Michigan
MISSISSIPPI STATE		Sept. 9	at Alabama
Aug. 31	South Carolina	Sept. 16	Arkansas
Sept. 9	Auburn	Sept. 23	Tennessee State
Sept. 16	Tulane	Sept. 30	Temple
Sept. 23	at UAB	Oct. 7	at Ole Miss
Sept. 30	at LSU	Oct. 14	at Georgia
Oct. 7	West Virginia	Oct. 28	at Duke
Oct. 14	Jacksonville State	Nov. 4	Florida
Oct. 21	at Georgia	Nov. 11	at Kentucky
Oct. 28	Kentucky	Nov. 18	Tennessee

NORTH VS. SOUTH:
How We Feel About Football

CAMPUS DECOR
North: Statues of founding fathers.
South: Statues of Heisman Trophy winners.

GETTING TO THE STADIUM
North : You ask "Where's the stadium?" When you find it, you walk right in.
South : When you're near it, you'll hear it. On game day, it becomes the state's third largest city.

PARKING
North : An hour before game time the university opens the campus for game parking.
South : RVs sporting school flags begin arriving on Wednesday for the weekend festivities.

HOMECOMING QUEEN
North : Also a physics major.
South : Also Miss USA.

ATTIRE
North : Men and women: woolly sweater or sweatshirt and jeans.
South : Men: pressed khakis, oxford shirt, cap with frat logo, Justin Ropers. Women: ankle-length skirt, coordinated cardigan, flat riding boots, oxford shirt.

WOMEN'S ACCESSORIES
North : Chapstick in her back pocket and a $20 bill in her front pocket.
South : Louis Vuitton duffel with two lipsticks, powder, mascara (waterproof), concealer, and a fifth of bourbon. Wallet not necessary; that's what dates are for.

TAILGATING
North : Raw meat on a grill, beer with lime in it, listening to local radio station with truck tailgate down.
South : 30-foot custom pig-shaped smoker fires up at dawn. Cooking accompanied by live performance by Jerry Jeff Walker, who comes over during breaks and asks for a hit off your bottle of bourbon.

CONCESSIONS
North : Drinks served in a paper cup filled to the top with soda.
South : Drinks served in a plastic cup imprinted with the home team's mascot, filled less than halfway to ensure enough room for bourbon.

WHEN THE NATIONAL ANTHEM IS PLAYED
North : Stands are less than half full.
South : 100,000 fans sing along in perfect three-part harmony.

THAT SMELL IN THE AIR AFTER THE FIRST SCORE
North : What smell?
South : Fireworks with a twist of bourbon.

AFTER THE GAME
North : The stadium is empty way before the game ends.
South : Another rack of ribs on the smoker. While somebody goes to the nearest package store for more bourbon, planning begins for next week's game.

SOUTHERNERS IN THE PRO FOOTBALL HALL OF FAME

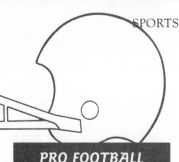

NAME	INDUCTED	BIRTHPLACE
Doug Atkins	1982	Humboldt, TN
Lem Barney	1992	Gulfport, MS
Bobby Bell	1983	Shelby, NC
Mel Blount	1989	Vidalia, GA
Terry Bradshaw	1989	Shreveport, LA
Jim Brown	1971	St Simons Island, GA
Roosevelt Brown	1975	Charlottesville, VA
Willie Brown	1984	Yazoo City, MS
Junious (Buck) Buchanan	1990	Gainesville, AL
Harry Carson	2006	Florence, SC
Willie Davis	1981	Lisbon, LA
Bill Dudley	1966	Bluefield, VA
Carl Eller	2004	Winston-Salem, NC
Frank Gatski	1985	Farmington, WV
Joe Gibbs	1996	Mocksville, NC
John Hannah	1991	Canton, GA
Paul Hornung	1986	Louisville, KY
Sam Huff	1982	Morgantown, WV
John Henry Johnson	1987	Waterproof, LA
Charlie Joiner	1996	Many, LA
Henry Jordan	1995	Emporia, VA
Sonny Jurgensen	1983	Wilmington, NC
Frank (Bruiser) Kinard	1971	Pelahatchie, MS
Willie Lanier	1986	Clover, VA
Larry Little	1993	Groveland, GA
Gino Marchetti	1972	Smithers, WV
George Preston Marshall	1963	Grafton, WV
George McAfee	1966	Corbin, KY
Marion Motley	1968	Leesburg, GA
Earle (Greasy) Neale	1969	Parkersburg, WV
Ozzie Newsome	1999	Muscle Shoals, AL
Clarence (Ace) Parker	1972	Portsmouth, VA
Jim Parker	1973	Macon, GA
Walter Payton	1993	Columbia, MS
Billy Shaw	1999	Natchez, MS
Art Shell	1989	Charleston, SC
Jackie Slater	20012	Jackson, MS
Jackie Smith	1994	Columbia, MS
John Stallworth	2002	Tuscaloosa, AL
Bart Starr	1977	Montgomery, AL
Dwight Stephenson	1998	Murfreesboro, NC
Lynn Swann	2001	Alcoa, TN
Fran Tarkenton	1986	Richmond, VA
Jim Taylor	1976	Baton Rouge, LA
Lawrence Taylor	1999	Williamsburg, VA
Reggie White	2006	Chattanooga, TN
Rayfield Wright	2006	Griffin, GA

PRO FOOTBALL IN THE SOUTH

ATLANTA FALCONS
Atlanta, GA
founded: 1966
Black, red, silver, white

CAROLINA PANTHERS
Charlotte, NC
founded: 1995
Black, Panther blue, silver

NEW ORLEANS SAINTS
New Orleans, LA
founded: 1967
Old gold, black, white

TENNESSEE TITANS
Nashville, TN
founded: 1960
Navy, Titans blue, white, red

COLLEGE BALL
SOUTHERN STYLE

SCHOOL	FOUNDED	ENROLLMENT	TEAM	COLORS
Alabama				
• Troy State Univ., Troy	1887	27,500	Trojans	Cardinal, silver, black
• Tuskegee University	1881	3,000	Golden Tigers	Crimson, gold, white
• University of Alabama, Tuscaloosa	1831	20,000	Crimson Tide	Crimson, white
• University of Auburn, Auburn	1856	24,000	Tigers	Burnt orange, navy
Arkansas				
• Arkansas State Univ., Jonesboro	1909	16,500	Indians	Red, black
• Univ. of Arkansas, Fayetteville	1871	18,000	Razorbacks	Cardinal red, white
Georgia				
• Georgia Tech, Atlanta	1885	15,000	Yellow Jackets	Old gold, white, navy
• Morehouse College, Atlanta	1867	3,000	Maroon Tigers	Maroon, white
• University of Georgia, Athens	1785	34,000	Bulldogs	Red, black
Kentucky				
• Morehead State Univ,. Morehead	1887	9,500	Eagles	Blue, gold
• Murray State Univ., Murray	1922	10,500	Racers	Navy blue, gold
• University of Kentucky, Lexington	1865	26,000	Wildcats	Blue, white
• University of Louisville, Louisville	1798	21,000	Cardinals	Red, black, white
Louisiana				
• Grambling State Univ.. Grambling	1901	8,000	Tigers	Black, gold
• Louisiana State (LSU). Baton Rouge	1860	32,000	Tigers	Purple, gold
• Tulane University. New Orleans	1834	11,500	Green Wave	Olive green, blue
Mississippi				
• Mississippi State Univ., Starkville	1878	16,000	Bulldogs	Maroon, white
• Univ. of Mississippi, Oxford	1844	16,500	Rebels	Red, blue

SCHOOL	FOUNDED	ENROLLMENT	TEAM	COLORS
North Carolina				
• Duke University, Durham	1838	12,500	Blue Devils	Blue, white
• NC State, Raleigh	1887	30,000	Wolfpack	Red, white
• University of NC, Chapel Hill	1789	26,000	Tar Heels	Powder blue, white
• Wake Forest Univ., Winston-Salem	1834	7,000	Demon Deacons	Gold, black
South Carolina				
• The Citadel, Charleston	1842	3,500	Bulldogs	Blue, white
• Clemson University	1889	17,000	Fighting Tigers	Burnt orange, purple
• Univ. of SC (USC), Columbia	1801	26,000	Gamecocks	Garnet, black
Tennessee				
• Tenn. State (TSU), Nashville	1912	9,000	Tigers	Blue, white
• Middle Tenn. State U. Murfreesboro	1911	22,000	Blue Raiders	Royal blue, white
• University of Memphis, Memphis	1912	21,000	Tigers	Blue, gray
• University of Tennessee, Knoxville	1794	26,000	Volunteers	Orange, white
• Vanderbilt University, Nashville	1873	6,500	Commodores	Black, gold
Virginia				
• Old Dominion Univ., Norfolk	1930	21,000	Monarchs	Slate blue, silver
• University of Virgini,a Charlottesville	1819	20,000	Cavaliers	Orange, blue
• Virginia Tech, Blacksburg	1872	28,000	Hokies	Burnt orange, maroon
West Virginia				
• West Va. University, Morgantown	1867	26,000	Mountaineers	Old gold, blue

What in the World is a HOKIE?

Virginia Tech has a made-up word for its team name. That's right. Way back in 1896, a contest was held to write a school cheer. The winner admitted the word—used in the cheer—was a product of his imagination, but the team has been the Hokies ever since. Yes, but what do they use as a mascot? A HokieBird (turkey), of course!

February 18, 2001

Dale Earnhardt, Sr.—called "The Intimidator" for his competitive fire and aggressive driving style—is an American auto racing legend. Quitting school at the age of 16 to pursue racing full time, he became one of NASCAR's greatest drivers. He clocked an amazing 76 career wins, and was best known for his driving in the Winston Cup series, in which he earned *seven* championships, beginning in 1975.

In 1951, Earnhardt was born to race car driver Ralph Earnhardt, and grew up with the sound of the race track in his ears. His first win came in 1979, when he was also named Rookie of the Year, dueling against legends Darrell Waltrip and Bobby Allison at Bristol Motor Speedway.

He earned the nickname "The Intimidator" during the Winston Cup at Charlotte, N.C. in his successful 1987 season, spinning out Bill Elliott in the final segment to take the first of his three career wins in the event. That year he recorded eleven wins across the country.

Talladega in 1996 was a close call for the fearless driver. When Ernie Irvan lost control of his Ford Thunderbird late in the race, Earnhardt, in the points lead, was caught in the wild crash and rocketed head-on into the wall at nearly 200 mph. His car flipped and slid across the track in front of race traffic. Earnhardt amazingly crawled out his car and waved to the crowd, despite a broken collarbone, sternum, and shoulder blade.

His great moment of glory came in 1998, when he won the Daytona 500 after 20 years. Ironically, it was in the Daytona 500 just three years later that Earnhardt was killed. By that time his son Dale Jr. was making a name for himself on the NASCAR circuit. Going into the final turn of the last lap, Michael Waltrip was leading Earnhart Jr., with Earnhardt Sr. in his famous #3 black car in third. As Sterling Marlin's car made contact from behind, Earnhardt Sr. spun out of control, and was then rammed by the oncoming car of Ken Shrader. Dale Earnhardt Sr. was pronounced dead when he was pulled from the wreck. It was February 18, 2001. Racing fans mourned the legend that so many had idolized. He meant so much, to so many.

Earnhardt was posthumously inducted into the International Motorsports Hall of Fame in 2006. Continuing in his father's footsteps, Dale Earnhardt Jr. won the Nextel Cup at the Daytona 500 in 2004. The legend continues.

The fatal crash on February 18, 2001.

NASCAR BY THE NUMBERS

- 43 cars are entered in each race.
- A driver can lose as much as 10 pounds during a race from dehydration.
- It can get as hot as 140 degrees F. inside the car.
- The pit crew consists of 7 members.
- A single tire weighs 75 pounds.
- The engines are 385 cubic inches and run about 780 horsepower.
- Race cars must weigh at least 3,400 pounds fully loaded.

What Is NASCAR?

National Association of Stock Car Auto Racing

They say that stock car racing was born in the bootlegging era (1920 to 1933)—and there's a considerable amount of truth in that—but the simple fact is, as soon as there were cars to drive, there were folks who wanted to race them. Daytona Beach, in that first decade of the 1900s, became the place to break land speed records, and in 1936 a course was created using the beach and Highway A1A, and racing events began to be held.

After watching unscrupulous promoters leave races without paying the drivers for a number of years, William France Sr. got together with influential racers and promoters to form NASCAR on February 21, 1948—to race "stock" (unmodified) cars. The first NASCAR stock car race ever was held at Charlotte Speedway on June 19, 1949.

NASCAR'S 50 GREATEST DRIVERS

As part of its fiftieth anniversary celebration, NASCAR named the fifty greatest drivers (as of 1998).

Bobby Allison	Ray Hendrick*	Richard Petty
Davey Allison*	Jack Ingram	Lee Petty
Buddy Baker	Bobby Isaac*	Tim Richmond*
Buck Baker	Ernie Irvan	Fireball Roberts*
Geoff Bodine	Dale Jarrett	Ricky Rudd
Neil Bonnett*	Ned Jarrett	Marshall Teague*
Red Byron*	Junior Johnson	Herb Thomas
Jerry Cook	Alan Kulwicki*	Curtis Turner*
Dale Earnhardt	Terry Labonte	Rusty Wallace
Ralph Earnhardt*	Fred Lorenzen	Darrell Waltrip
Bill Elliott	Tiny Lund*	Joe Weatherly*
Richie Evans*	Mark Martin	Bob Welborn*
Red Farmer	Hershel McGriff	Rex White
Tim Flock	Cotton Owens	Glen Wood
A.J. Foyt	Marvin Panch	Cale Yarborough
Harry Gant	Benny Parsons	LeeRoy Yarbrough*
Jeff Gordon	David Pearson	

*Deceased at time of the announcement.

KING RICHARD

Sixteen days after his twenty-first birthday, North Carolina native Richard Petty raced in his first NASCAR event (he was a second-generation racer: his father, Lee, won the first Daytona 500 in 1959). He went on to a remarkable career that earned him his nickname—the King—and earned him the respect of his racing peers and racing fans alike. Petty won seven series championships

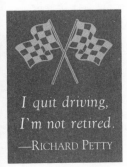

I quit driving,
I'm not retired.
—RICHARD PETTY

during his 35-year career, and in the most remarkable season in NASCAR history (1967), he won 27 of 48 races, including 10 consecutively, and placed second in seven more. In a career marked also by spectacular crashes, Petty's legacy is that of accessibility to the fans. Now retired, "King Richard" manages Petty Enterprises (which bears no alcohol decals or patches, due to a promise made to his mother) and is a national brand spokesman. Petty's son, Kyle, is also a well-known NASCAR driver.

NASCAR runs three main series of races:

- Nextel Cup
- Busch Series
- Craftsman Truck Series

NASCAR FLAGS

- Green: Indicates the race has started or restarted and cars are free to race.
- Yellow: Caution; cars slow and hold position. Indicates an unsafe racing condition.
- Red: Stop; all cars must stop on the track due to an unsafe condition.
- Black: Pull into the pits for consultation by a NASCAR official.
- Blue with orange stripe: Courtesy flag; move over for faster vehicle.
- White: Indicates the last lap of the race is underway.
- Checkered: The race has been completed. The first car to be shown this flag is the winner.

FOOD IS LOVE

Yes, Virginia, there really is such a thing as Southern hospitality. The phrase has come to mean an expansive, warm welcome into the home (no matter what part of the country one finds oneself in), but it has its basis in the South, where everyone smiles and nods or waves at passersby, and visitors are often treated to home-cooked meals.

The South on a Chain

Hungry for some good ol' Southern cuisine? You can probably find one of these Southern-based restaurants somewhere nearby:

- Cracker Barrel
- Hardee's
- Kentucky Fried Chicken
- Krispy Kreme
- Krystal
- Po' Folks
- Popeye's Chicken
- Shoney's
- Sonny's Real Pit Bar-B-Q
- Stuckey's
- Waffle House

In 1990, when the U.S. Navy's twelfth Trident nuclear submarine was christened the *U.S.S. Kentucky*, the bottle broken over its prow contained not champagne, but a special blend of eight kinds of Kentucky bourbon.

Nothing rekindles my spirits, gives comfort to my heart and mind, more than a visit to Mississippi ... and to be regaled as I often have been, with a platter of fried chicken, field peas, collard greens, fresh corn on the cob, sliced tomatoes with French dressing ... and to top it all off with a wedge of freshly baked pecan pie.

—CRAIG CLAIBORNE, in Southern Food

MAKE MINE ICED TEA!

No discussion of the South is complete without mentioning iced tea. We drink lots of it, and we drink it year-round. Order it in a restaurant, and it will come presweetened—what we call sweet tea. (If you prefer it otherwise, be sure to say so.) The first cold tea drinks—we find recipes for them in antique cookbooks from the mid-1800s—were served with plenty of alcohol, but today it's less common to use cold tea as a mixer.

Southern Sweet Tea

Pour 3 cups of boiling water over 3 to 4 teabags and allow to steep for 5 minutes. Add ¾ cup sugar to pitcher, then pour warm tea in, stirring to dissolve sugar. Add 5 cups of cold water and stir. Serve tea in tall glasses over large ice cubes. Garnish with lemon or lime.

Another Sweet Tea

Looking for something a little stronger? Try this iced tea cocktail!

¾ oz. dark rum
¾ oz. brandy
¾ oz. triple sec
¾ oz. orange juice

½ oz. lime juice
1 oz. cola
1 c. cold tea

Pour over crushed ice in a large highball glass, stir well, and serve. Garnish with lime wedge.

AMERICA'S NATIVE SPIRIT

That would be bourbon, which is a type of whiskey, made in America (and, more specifically, usually made in Kentucky!). You see, when the settlers pushed west past the Alleghenies into the glorious garden that is now Kentucky, they often passed through Bourbon County. In the vernacular of the day, the region became "Old Bourbon," and when supplies—very often whiskey—were shipped out of ports along the Ohio and Mississippi Rivers, they were stamped with their port of origin: "Old Bourbon." This whiskey was made from the fermentation of corn, and over time, bourbon came to be the name for a corn-based whiskey. In 1964, Congress in 1964 declared bourbon to be "America's Native Spirit" and its official distilled spirit. Here's to America!

THE JIM BEAM, WOODFORD RESERVE, AND JACK DANIELS DISTILLERIES ARE ALL LOCATED IN DRY COUNTIES!

TAKE A TOUR!

Currently operating whiskey distilleries that are open to the public include:

Jack Daniel's / Lynchburg, Tennessee

Jim Beam / Clermont, Kentucky

George Dickel / Tullahoma, Tennessee

Maker's Mark / Loretto, Kentucky

Wild Turkey / Lawrenceburg, Kentucky

Woodford Reserve / Versailles, Kentucky

─────── ⚜COVERED DISH ⚜ ───────

An integral part of Southern hospitality, the so-called covered dish appears on your doorstep when there's been a birth, a death, or other momentous event. Churches sponsor covered dish dinners (Yankees might call them pot-luck suppers), often once a week. A covered dish can be anything from a classic casserole to a plate of sliced, homegrown tomatoes—and anything in between!

EAT YOUR WAY TO PROSPERITY

If you eat poor on New Year's, you'll eat fat the rest of the year.

Many cultures believe what you do on New Year's Day sets the tone for the coming year, so here's the inside track on what to eat in the South on New Year's Day to ensure a year of happiness, prosperity, and good health.

Greens, black-eyed peas, rutabaga, sweet potatoes, pork, and rice are the common fare, with slight regional variations.

Hoppin' John (black-eyed peas and rice): The black-eyed peas represent coins. Simply mix cooked rice in with black-eyed peas that have been cooked with a ham hock.

Greens (usually collards or turnip greens): Greens represent paper money. Some cooks season them with fatback and sugar, or mix in a jar of homemade relish.

Pork: Pigs represent prosperity in many cultures. Pork can be served in many ways: roast, fatback ribs, or a ham hock cooked with black-eyed peas.

Starch (usually rice, potatoes, sweet potatoes or rutabagas): A symbol of abundance.

Corn bread: Well, no southern meal is complete without it!

CAJUN OR CREOLE?

Let's get one thing straight: they may hail from the same state, but these two types of food are not the same. New Orleans cooking style is Creole, not Cajun. And real Cajuns—the descendants of French Acadians who settled in southern Louisiana in the eighteenth century—don't eat blackened redfish. Or blackened anything. Sure, many Cajun dishes have a little kick to them; most dishes are seasoned with salt, black pepper, white pepper, and cayenne pepper. But the food you'll be served in Acadiana won't be eye-wateringly spicy hot.

An authentic Cajun meal is simple, even rustic. Folks outside Louisiana often confuse it with Creole cuisine, which was born in New Orleans and blends French, Spanish, French Caribbean, African, American and even Italian influences. Creole has its roots in classic European styles of cooking. Both types of cuisine adapted themselves to local ingredients and thus have similarities. Crawfish are a staple in both, as are the holy trinity of vegetables: onion, bell pepper, and celery. But red beans and rice? That's all Creole.

Honey, let's have Cajun tonight ...

• Comeaux's Café / 104 S. State St., Abbeville, LA 70510 / (337) 898-9218

"If you had a Cajun grandmother, this is how she cooked..."

• Préjean's Restaurant, 3480 U.S. Hwy. 167 No, Lafayette, LA 70507 (337) 896-7964

"Voted Acadiana's best Cajun food..."

Kigombo!

It's been said that gumbo is Louisiana's single most important culinary contribution to American kitchens, and it is a dish born from necessity: when French Acadians arrived in south Louisiana, they threw together a stew from local ingredients to imitate bouillabaisse, a seasoned fish stew. One local ingredient they found—and which is essential to gumbo— is okra. In fact, the word "gumbo" comes from an African word, *kigombo*, which means, well, okra.

So gumbo is a thick, hearty, seasoned stew. Composed of stock (liquid from simmered meat), okra, meat (can be crab, shrimp, chicken, oysters, or others), and vegetables (onions, celery, bell pepper, parsely, often tomatoes, and others), it's served over rice. Often, a roux is used as a thickening agent, although okra works quite well.

OKRA SHRIMP GUMBO

4 T. flour
⅛ c. oil
1 can whole tomatoes
4 stalks celery, chopped
1 lg. onion, chopped
1 bell pepper, chopped
¼ c. chopped shallots
2 lb. okra, sliced
3 lb. shrimp, peeled and deveined
4 qt. water
salt and pepper to taste
1 pt. shucked oysters
Cooked white rice

When the taste changes with every bite and the last bite is as good as the first, that's Cajun.
—PAUL PRUDHOMME, CHEF

In large pot over medium-high heat, make a roux of flour and oil, stirring until dark brown. Add celery, onion, pepper, and shallots to pot and cook until wilted. Fry okra in grease in separate pan; do not prepare ahead. Meanwhile, add shrimp to large pot and cook until pink. Add cooked okra; stir and simmer for five minutes, then add water and tomatoes to desired consistency. Add salt and pepper to taste; simmer, uncovered, for about 1-½ hours. Add oysters five minutes before serving.
Serve with boiled white rice.

The $105 Investment

World-famous Colonel Harland Sanders, known for his "finger lickin' good" Kentucky Fried Chicken, stands as a tribute to success coming late in life. Virtually penniless and living on Social Security at 65, Colonel Sanders turned his tasty fried chicken recipe into a worldwide franchise that is now one of the largest fast food corporations in the world.

Given the honorary title of Kentucky Colonel in 1935 by Governor Ruby Laffoon (when Sanders was 45) due to his delectable cooking skills, the spectacled Colonel Sanders was easily recognized by his southern gentleman dress—crisp white suit, black bowtie, and walking cane—and his signature moustache and goatee. He chose to dress the part of a southern gentleman in self-promotion, at which he excelled.

Born in September 1890, Sanders was the eldest of five children and learned to cook and take care of the family at the very tender age of six after his father died. Under his mother's direction, fried chicken became one his specialties.

Running a service station in Corbin, Kentucky, when he was 40, Sanders began providing meals for travelers, serving the diners in his own living room. As his popularity grew, he moved to a restaurant seating 142 people; his specialty, of course, was fried chicken, seasoned with his original blend of eleven secret herbs and spices.

Progress in the 1950s changed the tide of fortune for the Kentucky Colonel. A new highway, I-75, diverted traffic away from Corbin, and his successful business ended. His first Social Security check of $105 was a turning point. Determined not to spend the rest of his days sitting on the front porch in a rocking chair, Colonel Sanders brainstormed a plan and headed west with his chicken recipe and a dream.

Traveling across the country from restaurant to restaurant in 1952, the Colonel cooked batches of chicken for restaurant owners and their employees using his special recipe. If the reaction was favorable they entered a handshake agreement, guaranteeing the Colonel payment of a nickel per chicken sold. Thus Kentucky Fried Chicken was born. The first official franchise was set up in Salt Lake City, and today Kentucky Fried Chicken is served in over 80 countries. In 1964, Colonel Sanders sold his investment for $2 million dollars to a group of investors including John Y. Brown, who later became governor of Kentucky. In 1971, the company was sold again, to Heublein Inc., for $285 million!! Did the goose—oops, we mean chicken—lay the golden egg?

The Colonel died in 1980, at age 90, from leukemia; he was buried in his traditional white suit and black bowtie in Cave Hill Cemetery in Louisville, Kentucky, after lying in state in the rotunda of the Kentucky State Capitol. He is the only fast food franchiser honored with a bust in the state capitol. To this day, the recipe of eleven herbs and spices remains a trade secret.

Genuine Imitation Finger Lickin' Good Chicken

2 packages Italian salad dressing mix
3 tablespoons flour
2 teaspoons plus ½ teaspoon salt
¼ cup lemon juice
3 pounds chicken pieces, rinsed and patted dry
1 ½ cup pancake mix
Pepper to taste
Milk
Vegetable oil (for frying)

Mix the Italian salad dressing mix, flour, 2 teaspoons salt, and lemon juice until a paste forms. Coat the chicken evenly with this paste. Layer the chicken in a bowl and refrigerate for several hours, at least. When you are ready to cook the chicken, preheat the oven to 350 degrees F. Mix the pancake mix, ½ teaspoon salt, and pepper. Dip the chicken into the milk, and then dredge in the pancake mixture. Shake off the excess. In a large skillet containing ½ inch hot oil, lightly brown the chicken pieces in batches (about 4 minutes per side). Remove and place in a shallow baking dish. Cover with foil, and bake for 1 hour. Increase the oven temperature to 400 degrees F. Uncover, baste with fresh milk and continue baking for another 10 minutes, until crispy.

THE SOUTH'S MOST FAMOUS CULINARY EXPORT

Call it country fried chicken, call it southern fried chicken, or just called it fried chicken, this is a dish found on kitchen tables, on restaurant menus, and under warming tables in every other corner store in the South (remember, Col. Sanders first sold his from a gas station!). And, we might add, on tables across America ...

There are many ways to make southern fried chicken—some say the chicken should be dipped in a batter, some say it should simply be dredged in flour and seasonings, and others prefer the double dip method (into milk or other liquid first, then in dry flour). With skin or without? That's another question sure to provoke a lively debate. Fry in oil, butter, or grease? It seems everyone's idea of "real" southern fried chicken depends a lot on where we grew up. However, there's one thing all Southerners agree on: the chicken must be fried in a cast-iron skillet. And honey, we do not pull our fried chicken apart with a fork—fried chicken is finger food!

SUPPER OR DINNER?

THERE'S A LOT OF CONFUSION ABOUT THE USAGE OF THESE WORDS, AND IN MANY PARTS OF THE COUNTRY THEY'VE BECOME INTERCHANGEABLE, BUT IF THE SPEAKER HAILS FROM THE SOUTH, THERE'S NO QUESTION: DINNER REFERS TO THE LARGE MIDDAY MEAL, AND SUPPER IS WHAT YOU EAT IN THE EVENING.

First, you need a cast-iron skillet ...

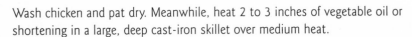

INGREDIENTS:
5–6 lbs. chicken pieces
2 c. flour
I tsp. salt
½ tsp. pepper
I c. milk
vegetable oil or shortening for frying

Wash chicken and pat dry. Meanwhile, heat 2 to 3 inches of vegetable oil or shortening in a large, deep cast-iron skillet over medium heat.

In a heavy brown paper bag, combine the flour, salt, and pepper; shake to blend well.

When oil is hot (test by shaking a drop of water into the oil; it should spatter immediately), dip a few pieces of chicken in milk, then shake in the bag (this coats it evenly and lightly). Place chicken in skillet; do not overcrowd.

Fry the chicken until golden brown and crisp, about 15 to 20 minutes, turning once to brown both sides. Reduce heat and continue frying until cooked through, about 15 minutes longer.

Drain chicken on brown paper or paper towels, then transfer to platter. Serves 8.

Now, hush up puppy!

Yes, we love fried foods. If it can be battered, we'll fry it, and that goes for green tomatoes, pickles, chopped steak, okra, squash, even French fries! We'll even fry the batter by itself—can you say "funnel cake"?

But best of all, we love fried catfish and hushpuppies! Whether the fish came out of the pond out back, or from the grocery store, there's no meal quite as Southern as fried catfish.

Hushpuppies—made from cornmeal, flour, eggs, salt, baking soda, milk, and chopped onions, dropped by dollops into hot grease—were historically made from the leftover batter and were fed to the family hound.

MAKE MINE COUNTRY

The cuisine of the South draws heavily on local ingredients and influences from ethnic groups that have lived here. We call it "home" or "country" cookin' —food that folks outside the region often refer to as soul food. And while the so-called soul foods often had their roots in Africa, there are other influences to note: for example, Native Americans brought squash, tomatoes, and corn (and the many dishes derived from corn, such as grits and cornbread) to the table. The practice of roasting meat in a deep pit also came from Native Americans, while dishes requiring eggs, sugar, milk, and flour often originated in Europe. The fact that your granny served you a huge breakfast probably has its genesis in the British Isles, where they love a big "fry up" in the morning. Of course, our moonshine tradition is derived from Scot/Irish settlers, who brought experience in distilling with them. Whatever you call it, it's *good!*

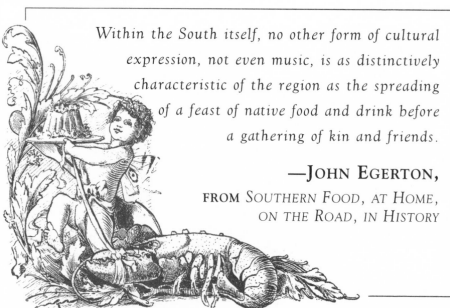

Within the South itself, no other form of cultural expression, not even music, is as distinctively characteristic of the region as the spreading of a feast of native food and drink before a gathering of kin and friends.

—JOHN EGERTON,
FROM SOUTHERN FOOD, AT HOME,
ON THE ROAD, IN HISTORY

Good Country Cookin'

Recreating the heart and soul of yesteryear's old country store, Dan Evins created one of the country's most successful restaurant chains when he opened the first Cracker Barrel Old Country Store on September 19, 1969. Evins combined the appeal of the country store as the local gathering place with a desire to provide good quality, simple country food. Southerners ate it up (so to speak).

With that flush of success, the company went public on the stock exchange in 1981, and that same year was sited one of the nation's foremost growth chains in *Institutions Magazine.* Today there are 538 stores in 41 states coast-to-coast, well known for the downhome country cooking and daily made-from-scratch biscuits. The cornbread is made from an old country recipe, and their maple syrup comes from real maple trees in Vermont. If you don't like the food (gasp!!), then set a spell to play some checkers.

In a typical year Cracker Barrel serves:
- 35 million bottles of maple syrup (6% of the world's supply!)
- 114 million slices of bacon
- 127 million eggs
- 18 million orders of Chicken 'n' Dumplins

In 2005 Cracker Barrel sold enough pancake mix to make 8 million pancakes. That's a stack of pancakes 31 miles high.

THE DIFFERENCE BETWEEN GRILLING AND BARBEQUE

There's a lot of semantic confusion centering around the word *barbeque*, so let's clear that up right now. A lot of the confusion comes from the fact that oftentimes the same piece of equipment is used to grill or to barbeque. Simply put, grilling is a high, direct heat method. You grill hamburgers. Barbeque involves low, indirect heat and smoking to cook the meat.

So even though Yankees might say—and we've heard 'em say it!—"We're going to barbeque hamburgers tonight," that's actually incorrect. (Aussies, we've heard, actually call the *grill* a barbeque, and that, too, is incorrect, mate.) And there's so much more than that ... because in the South, barbeque is not only a verb. It's a noun, too ...

You might hear "I'm going to run out to the Happy Piggy and pick up a couple pounds of barbeque," which means that we're having smoked pork for supper. But don't describe a gathering of folks standing around on the patio, beers in hand, watching a guy in a "Kiss the Cook" apron grill steaks or hamburgers as "going to a barbeque!" That's a cook-out!

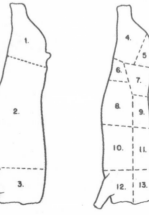

1. Gammon
2. Middle
3. Fore end
4. Gammon hock
5. Corner gammon
6. Flank
7. Long loin
8. Thin streaky
9. Short back
10. Thick streaky
11. Rib back
12. Forehock
13. Collar

BARBEQUE BY THE REGION

When Southerners talk about barbeque, we mean pork. Oh sure, there've been a few experiments … we hear that Texans do well by beef brisket, for example. But in Dixie, we're talkin' about the hog. And that's where the similarities cease! Region by region, seasonings and sauces (not to mention side dishes) are sometimes dramatically different! There are basically four types (listed in order of evolution):

- **peppery vinegar sauce** (mostly found in eastern North Carolina)
- **peppery vinegar sauce with tomato ketchup added** (moving west in North Carolina into East Tennessee)
- **mustard-based sauce with vinegar and ketchup** (South Carolina)
- **tomato-based** (everywhere else)
  Tomato-based sauces can be sweet, smoky, spicy or a combination of all three.

"BARBECUE THOUGH THE AGES"

"Spare rib, anyone?"
—ADAM

"The right mood music is an essential part of a good barbecue party."
—NERO

"It is better to have burnt and lost, then never to have grilled at all."
—WILLIAM SHAKESPEARE

"L'Angleterre est une nation de barbecuers."
—NAPOLEON BONAPARTE

"It is a far, far better barbecue that I have now than I have ever had before."
—CHARLES DICKENS, *A TALE OF TWO CITIES*

"Barbecuing is one percent inspiration, and ninety-nine percent perspiration."
—THOMAS EDISON

"The larger the mass of food, the more energy it will take to cook. This energy should be distributed over a larger time period or the surface of the food will receive a disproportionate amount of that energy."
—ALBERT EINSTEIN

Going Whole Hog

How to Roast a Pig

Naw, we're not talking about giving politicians a hard time. We're talking about pork, pigs, hogs, our porcine friends, loafers on the hoof. If you've never been to or hosted a pig roast, there's nothing to it!! The nice folks at The National Pork Board have put together these tips, though they may not have phrased it *exactly* this way... (Note, this list is not necessarily complete, so if you're serious about this, do a little research.)

1) Pick Yer Pig

This is something that most people will want to buy. It's called a "dressed" pig, but it's really undressed (that is, gutted and cleaned but with head, skin, bones, and feet intact; it should be opened butterfly-fashion). Contact a specialty butcher, or your local grocery store; they will often order one for you. A 75-pound dressed pig will yield about 30 pounds of cooked pork, and for serving portions, figure about one pound per person. More if you like them.

2) Clear Your Calendar

Roasting a whole pig takes time. Lots of time. Don't plan to go anywhere for several hours. One estimate is at least 4 hours for a 75-pound live weight. When in doubt, plan to leave the pig in longer. Additional cooking won't hurt it, as it's really being steamed.

3) Dig the Pit

— dig a hole about 3 feet deep at the center, with a diameter of 5 to 7 feet, depending on the size of the pig

— line the pit with rocks

— light a fire (usually charcoal, about 40 pounds for a 50-pound pig)

— put more, smaller rocks in the fire pit to heat

— as the fire burns down, wet down some burlap, and prepare the pig as desired (seasonings, basting sauces, etc.)

— grab your buddies, and hoist that baby onto some chicken wire (large enough to hold the pig)

   — make some slits under the legs, large enough to insert the hot rocks

   — fill the abdominal cavity and the slits under the legs with hot rocks (don't use bare hands)

   — tie the front legs together, then tie the back legs together

   — wrap the chicken wire around the pig, fastening so it can be lifted

— cover the ashed coals and rocks with corn stalks, or leaves, or grass trimmings

— lower the chicken-wire-wrapped pig onto the leaves

— top the pig with more stalks, leaves, or grass trimmings

— put the wet burlap over the leaves to hold in the heat

— cover it all with a large, heavy canvas

— shovel dirt or gravel over the top to keep the heat in

4) Cook Yer Pig

Estimate the cooking time; depending on cooking times, this could mean starting cooking about 12 hours before your event. When the pig reaches an internal temperature of 160 degrees F., remove the pig from the heat. It will hold for about 1-2 hours without drying out.

5) Think Again

On second thought, you may just want to eat out.

Wall Street got its name when colonial Manhattan residents blocked free-roaming hogs from entering modern-day Lower Manhattan by building a long, permanent wall. Eventually, a street came to border this wall—Wall Street.

In seventeenth century England, a "pig in a poke" was a trick sometimes played upon unsuspecting shoppers by substituting a cat for a suckling pig. When the buyer opened the poke (sack), he "let the cat out of the bag," and revealed the scam.

Beer, Politics, and Fish

The tradition of shad planking dates before the Revolutionary War, when shad were plentiful along Virginian shores. The male buck shad, weighing two to three pounds, swims upriver followed by the large roes, or females, which weigh seven or eight pounds. When the water temperature rises above 60 degrees, the fish spawn and return to the ocean.

An easy catch for fishermen, both flesh and roe (eggs) of shad are eaten. They are cleaned, split open, then nailed flat to the oak boards (hence the name planking), and smoked, turning several times. It's often basted with a "secret" sauce. The shad planking celebrated every April in Wakefield, Virginia, began in the 1930s to mark the start of the fishing season and the running of the shad up the James River. Learning from similar traditions in the rest of the South, the community adopted the tradition as an annual fund-raising event, which soon grew into a political gossip festival. It became *the* place to see and be seen, with politicians giving casual and entertaining speeches.

Shad planking in Wakefield is now as steeped in tradition as Virginia politics and the two are inextricably entwined. Every spring the crowd comes for the oily fish, beer, and for the political meet-and-greet.

BAKED SHAD ROE
Bacon slices

1 set shad roe per person

Preheat oven to 400 degrees F. Cut bacon slices lengthwise, and place a slice under each half of the shad roe. Cut more bacon into small pieces and scatter on top of the roe. Bake 25 to30 minutes or until done.

The largest member of the herring family, shad are anadromous fish, meaning they are born in fresh water, migrate to the ocean to grow into adults, and then return to fresh water to spawn.

HUNTING THE WILY RAMP

Ever eat a ramp? Some parts are edible (to paraphrase Euell Gibbons, father of the back-to-nature movement and the authority on wild edible plants). The ramp (*Allium tricoccum*), or wild leek, belongs to the same family as onions and chives, and can be found in woodlands and forests ranging through the Appalachians from West Virginia to Georgia.

Considered a Southern delicacy announcing the arrival of spring, ramp festivals are held in numerous small towns throughout Appalachia, where the pungent wild greens may be eaten pickled, raw, fried, or cooked in soups, casseroles, or puddings. The bulbs are spicy, like a cross between garlic and scallions. Due to their strong aftertaste and pungent odor that exudes from the skin for several days after eating them, it's best to eat ramps at the same time that your family or friends do!

The name "ramp" is an adaptation of an Elizabethan word used for wild garlic (hramsa), shortened by early settlers in the Appalachians to "ramp."

Ramps grow in large colonies in rich, moist, deciduous forests, emerging in late March and early April in cool, shady areas. Each bulb shoots up two or three broad leaves that grow 8-12 inches tall. When the forest canopy begins to shade out the summer sun, the leaves wither and die, leaving a single bud on a naked stalk. The plant goes into dormancy after producing a small cluster of flowers and seed capsule, reemerging the following spring.

If you don't have ramps growing in woods nearby, they can be found in some gourmet food outlets or from Earthy Delights (along with other unusual foodstuffs; call 800-367-4709 or visit the Web at www.earthy.com).

ꓛTATO & RAMP SOUP

slices bacon, crisply fried and
ᴜmbled (reserve bacon fat)
cups cleaned, chopped ramps (green part included)
cups diced red potatoes
tablespoons flour
cups chicken broth
cup heavy cream
ᴏalt and pepper to taste

ın a large Dutch oven or skillet, fry the ramps and potatoes in the bacon fat until ramps are tender. Sprinkle with the flour and stir until the flour is absorbed. Stir in the chicken broth and simmer until the potatoes are tender. Stir in the cream and heat thoroughly. Salt and pepper to taste and top with the crumbled bacon. Serves about 4 to 6 dedicated ramp lovers.

MARTHA WHITE'S FINEST HOUR

Some form of biscuits has been around for centuries, but it was the South that raised the lowly biscuit to high art. In the rural Old South, children were fed an early meal of biscuits and molasses or sorghum syrup. Dry, day-old biscuits might be crumbled in milk or buttermilk and drizzled with honey, or perhaps a slice of ham, bacon, or sausage might be slipped between a sliced biscuit. Best of all, Mama might whip up a thick country gravy, and ladle it over a split biscuit—a breakfast that would stick to your ribs for hours. A big basket of biscuits would accompany the large midday meal and supper, as it does today. Buttermilk makes a biscuit particularly light and flakey, so we're sharing our buttermilk biscuit recipe here. The term "cathead" refers to the size of the biscuit when it's cut into large rounds—as large as a cat's head!

Buttermilk Cathead Biscuits

3 c. all-purpose flour
3 tsp. baking powder
1 tsp. salt
¾ tsp. baking soda
¾ c. shortening
¾ c. buttermilk

Preheat oven 450 degrees F. Mix dry ingredients and sift twice. In large bowl, cut shortening into flour until mixture forms coarse crumbs, then add buttermilk gradually to form a soft dough. Turn dough onto floured surface and knead by hand until smooth, then roll dough until it's ½-inch thick. Cut with floured round cutter, and place biscuits, lightly touching, on ungreased baking sheet. Bake for 12 to 15 minutes, until golden on top. Just like Grandma used to make!

SOUTHERN CORNBREAD

Native Americans were grinding corn and making a form of cornbread long before the European settlers arrived. Lucky for us, the settlers paid close attention to those early cooks! Called by a variety of names—johnnycake, cornpone, hoecake, and plain ol' cornbread—this quick bread is a fixture on any Southern table.

Early forms of cornbread were fried on a griddle (similar to a pancake) but traditional Southern cornbread today is baked in a cast-iron skillet (sometimes it's baked as muffins, or poured into molds that produce cornbread "sticks"). Made with white cornmeal, Southern cornbread is *not* sweet, unlike Yankee cornbread.

Like biscuits, cornbread can be found at just about any meal in the South. Spread with butter and honey it's a delightful breakfast, crumbled over a bowl of beans it's a filling meal … and sometimes you'll see it alongside collard or turnip greens, where it's used to sop up the liquid.

Sometimes we add other ingredients, like shredded cheese, whole kernel corn, or hot peppers—cornbread is a willing base for any number of interesting additions. (We like chopped onions and black olives.) Ask a dozen Southern cooks for a cornbread recipe, and you're likely to get a dozen different recipes—but none of those recipes will have sugar, and all of them will require a preheated cast-iron skillet!

Real Southern Cornbread

2 tbsp. bacon drippings
2 c. white cornmeal
4 tsp. baking powder
1 tsp. salt
2 eggs, beaten
2 c. buttermilk

Preheat oven to 450 degrees F. Place bacon drippings in 9-inch cast-iron skillet and put in oven to heat. Combine dry ingredients, then add eggs and buttermilk; mix well. Pour into hot pan with bacon drippings (batter will sizzle). Bake for 35 minutes or until golden brown. Serves 6 to 8.

FRIED GREEN TOMATOES

As a culinary delicacy, fried green tomatoes simply can't be beat. There are two basic batters—cornmeal or flour—just use the one you prefer (the recipe is the same).

Fried Green Tomatoes (Cornmeal)

4 to 6 green tomatoes

Salt and pepper

Cornmeal

Bacon grease

Slice tomatoes into ½-inch slices; salt and pepper to taste. Dip in cornmeal and fry in hot grease about 3 minutes or until golden on bottom. Flip carefully and fry the other side. Remove to paper towel to drain before serving.

TRIVIA

It is commonly accepted that the inspiration for the café in Fanny Flagg's novel *Fried Green Tomatoes at the Whistle Stop Café* is the real-life Irondale Cafe, located in the northeastern Birmingham town of Irondale. Fried green tomatoes are a specialty of the house.

Test Your Southern IQ

Naw, this isn't a test of how book smart you are, it's just a fun quiz to see how southern you really, really are.

What's it called when you wade into deep water, stick your hand into a hollow, submerged log, and try to grab a catfish?

   Noodling (Some might call it stupid.)

How many Vienna sausages are in a can?

   Seven

If you crossed a heifer and a steer, what would you get?

   Ha! Nothing. (It's a trick—a steer has been castrated. Ouch.)

Goober Peas

Although we call them peaNUTs, they are not technically a nut, but a woody legume. But we don't care what you call them— roasted and salted, you can't beat this relative of the pea for pure crunching pleasure. Domesticated in South America, they're ideally suited to cultivation in the South, where they easily receive several months of warm weather along with ample rain.

The first commercial crops of peanuts were grown in the early 1800s in Virginia and North Carolina, but it took the Civil War to bring the peanut to the attention of a larger audience. As the war dragged on, diminishing the resources of both armies, soldiers foraging for any potential food source discovered the tasty, nutritious legume; Union soldiers returning home spread news of the peanut far and wide. By the 1890s, a St. Louis doctor had invented peanut butter, and the rest, as they say, is history. Peanuts are also known as earthnuts, goobers (or goober peas), pindas, jack nuts, pinders, manila nuts, and monkey nuts.

"AN ARMY MARCHES ON ITS STOMACH"

Napoleon Bonaparte uttered those famous words, but it was the Confederate Army that embodied them—giving us a popular camp song still in use today. First editions of the song appeared as the war ended, crediting the words to "A. Pindar, Esq." and the music to "P. Nutt, Esq." Every Southerner saw the joke immediately.

"Goober Peas"

Sitting by the roadside on a
   summer's day
Chatting with my mess-mates,
   passing time away
Lying in the shadows underneath
   the trees
Goodness, how delicious, eating
   goober peas.

CHORUS
Peas, peas, peas, peas
Eating goober peas
Goodness, how delicious,
Eating goober peas.

When a horseman passes, the soldiers
   have a rule
To cry out their loudest, "Mister, here's your
   mule!"

But another custom, enchanting-er than these
   Is wearing out your grinders, eating goober peas.

CHORUS

Just before the battle, the General hears a row
   He says "The Yanks are coming, I hear their
   rifles now."
He looks down the roadway, and what d'ya
   think he sees?
   The Georgia Militia cracking goober peas.

CHORUS

   I think my song has lasted just about
   enough.
   The subject is interesting, but the
   rhymes are mighty rough.
I wish the war was over, so free
   from rags and fleas
We'd kiss our wives and sweethearts,
   say good-bye to goober peas.

CHORUS

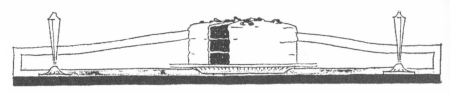

The Sweetest Thing

No Southern meal is complete without dessert, and Southern cooks are known for their cakes and pies (especially ones that feature fruit). Here are some of our favorite sweet treats:

Red Velvet Cake

Although some recipes may call for red food coloring, it's the acidic reaction of the vinegar and buttermilk with cocoa that turns the cake a reddish color. If you prefer a more dramatic color, add 2 tbsp. of red food coloring.

Softened butter for the pans
2-½ c. flour
1-½ c. sugar
1 tsp. baking soda
1 tsp. salt
1 tsp. cocoa powder
1-½ c. vegetable oil
1 c. buttermilk, at room temperature
2 large eggs, at room temperature
1 tsp. white distilled vinegar
1 tsp. vanilla extract

Preheat oven to 350 degrees F. Lightly butter and flour three 9-inch round cake pans. In large bowl, sift together flour, sugar, baking soda, salt, and cocoa powder. In another large bowl, whisk together the oil, buttermilk, eggs, vinegar, and vanilla. Mix the dry ingredients into the wet ingredients until a smooth batter is formed.

Cream Cheese Frosting

1 pound cream cheese, softened
4 c. sifted confectioners' sugar
1 c. unsalted butter, softened
1 tsp. vanilla extract

Mix the cream cheese, sugar, and butter on low speed until combined, then increase speed to high, and mix until light and fluffy, about 5 minutes. Add vanilla gradually and mix briefly until fluffy.

Divide the cake batter evenly among the prepared cake pans and place in oven evenly spaced apart. Bake until a toothpick inserted in the center of the cakes comes out clean, about 30 minutes. Let cool completely before frosting with cream cheese frosting.

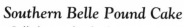

Southern Belle Pound Cake

Called pound cake because original recipes measured every-thing in pounds ... or perhaps it's because the finished cake is so rich and heavy! Serve with seasonal fresh fruit and whipped cream, or just enjoy it plain.

Softened butter for the pan	2-¼ c. sugar
3 c. flour	1 lb. butter, softened
½ tsp. baking soda	6 large eggs
1 tsp. baking powder	½ c. buttermilk
½ tsp. salt	2 tsp. vanilla extract

Preheat oven to 325 degrees F. Butter and flour a standard tube pan. Sift flour, baking soda, and baking powder into a large mixing bowl. With wooden spoon, stir in salt and sugar. Fold in butter, then eggs. Using a mixer, gradually add buttermilk and vanilla; if mixture is thick, add extra buttermilk, a tablespoon at a time. Whip thoroughly, then pour batter into cake pan. Bake for about 1 hour and 20 minutes, or until a toothpick inserted in the center comes out dry. Be careful not to jar the cake, as it can collapse. Allow cake to cool completely before inverting pan onto cake plate.

Fruit Cobbler

Cobblers are a deep-dish fruit dessert made with fruit or berries and a basic biscuit crust. Traditionally served hot out of the oven, they're especially good with a dollop of vanilla ice cream on top!

½ c. butter
1 c. flour
1 c. sugar
1 tsp. baking powder
1 c. milk
1 (21 ounce) can pie filling (any fruit*)

Preheat oven to 350 degrees F. Melt butter in 9x13 inch pan as oven preheats. In a medium bowl, mix together flour, sugar, and baking powder. Stir in milk. Remove pan of melted butter or margarine from oven. Pour mixture into pan, but do not stir. Spread pie filling onto batter, also without stirring. Bake for 50 to 60 minutes, until fruit is bubbly and batter is set and golden brown.

*Want to use fresh? Substitute 2 cups fresh, ripe fruit in season, peeled and sliced if necessary. Southern cooks love to use blackberries, cherries, peaches, blueberries, even apples. Sometimes raisins are added to a peach or apple cobbler.

Mississippi Mud Cake

The marshmallow creme indicates that this cake was "invented" after World War II, although the notion of a thick, gooey chocolate cake is much older. We don't care—this is one of our favorites!

1 c. butter	1-½ c. flour
2 c. sugar	½ tsp. baking powder
½ c. cocoa	1 c. coconut
4 eggs	1 c. chopped pecans
1 tsp. vanilla	1 jar (7 oz.) marshmallow creme

Preheat oven to 350 degrees F. Grease and flour a 9x13 pan. In a large mixing bowl, cream together butter, sugar, and cocoa. Add eggs and vanilla, mix well. Add flour, baking powder, coconut, and nuts; beat for about two minutes. Spread batter in pan; bake for 30 minutes, then remove from oven. Poke holes in cake with handle of wooden spoon and spread marshmallow creme over the top while the cake is still hot. Cool and frost (recipe below). Store in the refrigerator.

Mud Cake Frosting

3 c. powdered sugar, sifted
½ c. butter or margarine
⅓ c. cocoa
½ c. evaporated milk

Whip together in order listed; add milk gradually until desired consistency is reached. Spread on cooled cake.

Classic Southern Pecan Pie

This is the desert most often associated with the South. Although we assume that early settlers made some variant of a pecan pie, the process for refining corn sugar—a primary ingredient—was not developed until the 1880s, and the earliest we see a recipe in print is 1925. Who cares? Let's have a slice now!

3 eggs, lightly beaten
1 c. corn syrup
1 c. sugar
2 tbsp. butter, melted
1 tsp. vanilla
1-½ c. pecan pieces
1 unbaked 9-inch pastry shell

Preheat oven to 350 degrees F. In large bowl, stir eggs, corn syrup, sugar, butter, and vanilla until well blended. Add nuts, stir, and pour into pastry shell. Bake 50 to 55 minutes, or until knife inserted halfway between the edge and center of pie comes out clean. Cool and serve with whipped cream.

Pastry

2 c. flour
1-½ tsp. salt
¼ c. cold milk
½ c. vegetable oil

Sift flour and salt together. Pour milk and oil together but do not mix; add all at once to flour mixture and stir lightly with a fork. Roll out on floured board, then place carefully in pie tin and cut edges to fit.

Georgia pecan wood was chosen for the handles of the Olympic relay torches for the 1996 Olympic Games in Atlanta.

It would take 97,182,000 pecan pies to circle the Earth, assuming each pie is 9 inches in diameter.

The official state "nut" of Alabama is the pecan (we know what you're thinking....)

The world's largest pecan tree nursery is in Lumberton, Mississippi.

MORE SOUTHERN TREATS!

A Little of This, A Little of That...
Western Kentucky Burgoo

Simply put, it's a stew. And it's a stew without an official recipe—every Kentuckian who cooks burgoo uses a recipe passed down through friends or family, and guards that recipe fiercely.

A descendant of the Irish mulligan stew (in which the ingredients were whatever came to hand), we find the first mention of burgoo in *Adventures by Sea*, by Edward Coxere, published around 1650. It was a favorite of sailors who thickened it with oatmeal or bulghur wheat. As settlers retired from the sea and moved inland, local ingredients were used to make this filling stew. Today thickening agents such as okra, whole wheat, cornmeal, or ground beans are often used.

And that's the thing—the recipe consists of four basic ingredients: meat, vegetables, a thickening agent, and savory spices. There is a fifth element though: time. Most burgoos are cooked—often in huge pots—for 24 or more hours. Ingredients are added in the order that it takes them to cook, thus the meat is added first, veggies next, and thickening agents last. Meats are often combined: beef, pork, chicken, mutton, even game meats. Vegetables include potatoes, carrots, tomatoes, lima beans, corn, green beans, and onions. Spices and herbs include salt, pepper, garlic, oregano, basil, tarragon, nutmeg, paprika, even cinnamon in some regions.

Even the side items vary from county to county—some serve cornbread or corn muffins, others a slice of white bread, and at the Kentucky Derby, where it is a tradition, it is served with saltine crackers.

TRIVIA

Interestingly, diners can often find burgoo served at barbeque restaurants in Kentucky! Don't ask us why ...

> ## WANT TO TRY SOME BURGOO?
> ## CHECK OUT THESE EVENTS!
>
> - ANDERSON COUNTY BURGOO FESTIVAL (late September)
>   Lawrenceburg, KY
>
> - BLUEGRASS, BURGOO, AND BARBECUE FESTIVAL (mid-September)
>   Winchester, KY
>
> - BURGOO INTERNATIONAL COOK-OFF (early October)
>   Webster Springs, WV

What's a GooGoo?

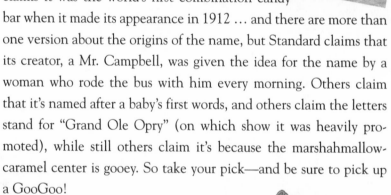

Visitors to Tennessee invariably come across a GooGoo Cluster at the convenience store, and want to know what it is. The Standard Candy Company, maker of the GooGoo, claims it was the world's first combination candy bar when it made its appearance in 1912 ... and there are more than one version about the origins of the name, but Standard claims that its creator, a Mr. Campbell, was given the idea for the name by a woman who rode the bus with him every morning. Others claim that it's named after a baby's first words, and others claim the letters stand for "Grand Ole Opry" (on which show it was heavily promoted), while still others claim it's because the marshahmallow-caramel center is gooey. So take your pick—and be sure to pick up a GooGoo!

Tastes Better Than It Sounds!

You know you're in the South when you see someone having Coke-n-peanuts ... pour a pack of salted peanuts into your Coke, and munch a few peanuts with every swallow. It's a taste treat!

Let's Go to the Beach!

VIRGINIA
Virginia Beach
The city of Virginia Beach is listed in *Guinness World Records* as having the longest pleasure beach in the world. The Virginia Aquarium and the Back Bay National Wildlife Refuge are nearby.

NORTH CAROLINA
The Outer Banks
A string of narrow barrier islands just off the cost of North Carolina, the Outer Banks include miles of flawless beaches. Some villages are accessible only by 4-wheel drive. Observe wildlife at several national parks and wildlife refuges.

SOUTH CAROLINA
Kiawah Island
Check out this semitropical island with ten miles of pristine beaches (to enjoy the beaches you'll need to rent a vacation condo or cottage). You'll want to visit Charleston, too, just 21 miles away.

GEORGIA
Tybee Island
A quiet getaway just outside Savannah, Tybee Island has 5 miles of lovely beaches and protected dunes. Take a dolphin-sighting tour, visit historic Fort Pulaski, and be sure you spend some time in Savannah when you come.

ALABAMA
Gulf Shores
Making a comeback from Hurricane Ivan, Alabama's Gulf Coast has miles of popular public beaches. Be sure to visit the Estuarium at the Dauphin Island Sea Lab or the Bon Secour Wildlife Preserve.

MISSISSIPPI
Biloxi
Often called the Southern Riviera, the 26 miles of beach were severely damaged by the 30-foot storm surge created by Hurricane Katrina. As of this writing Biloxi is still recovering, but tourism will help.

THERE'S A FUNGUS AMONG US
Hunting the Spring Morel

Morels are cone-shaped mushrooms, with a distinctive honeycomb-like cap. Like all mushrooms, they are the reproductive parts of a mycelium that grows underground. Morels are much prized by collectors, who liken them to truffles. Morels are hunted in early spring, usually following cold, rainy weather. At the first breath of warmer weather (we're talking the 50s), morel hunters are in the field, searching woodland areas. Some say that south-facing slopes are the best locations to spot morels. But even if you don't find any morels, at the very least you'll have a great walk outdoors in the spring. And there's nothing finer than springtime in the South.

Warning

It's no joke to eat a poisonous mushroom. Before you embark on the great morel hunt, contact some local 'shroomers to make absolutely sure you know what you're looking for. There are clubs, believe it or not. If in doubt, throw it out. (There's a reason why we didn't put this page in the Cooking chapter....)

Southerners love gardens. From the local garden club ladies to the good ol' boys growing a few 'maters out back, just about everyone you meet has a touch of the green thumb. And why not? With our long growing season and mild winters, the South is a great place to garden. Here are some beautiful public gardens to enjoy.

Bellingrath Gardens and Home *(Admission)*
12401 Bellingrath Rd., Theodore, AL 36582 (251) 973-2217
Sixty-five acres among towering live oaks draped in Spanish moss were landscaped in the 1920s. Points of interest include formal gardens, rose garden, riverfront walk, rockery, butterfly garden, conservatory, nature walk, and bayou boardwalk. And that's before you visit the home.

Bernheim Arboretum *(Admission on weekends & holidays; otherwise, free)*
State Highway 245, P. O. Box 130, Clermont, KY 40110 / (502) 955-8512
Within the 14,000 acre site, visitors will find a nationally recognized arboretum, a research forest, beautiful gardens, and 35 miles of hiking trails.

Bog Garden *(Free)*
1101 Hobbs Rd., Greensboro, NC 237403 / (335) 373-2199
This nature preserve, botanical garden, and city park features a bog and lake viewed from an elevated boardwalk. A haven for native and migratory birds, the site includes indigenous wildflowers and wild roses, ferns, and individually labeled trees.

Callaway Gardens *(Admission)*
205 N. Cherry Ave., Pine Mountain, GA 31822 (706) 663-2281
Grounds encompass gardens, woodland, a beach, resort, chapel, and championship golf course on a 13,000-acre nature preserve. Includes hiking trails to appreciate specialty gardens such as holly, azaleas (including the rare wild prunifolia azalea), rhododendrons, wildflowers, and more. Also includes an enclosed tropical butterfly conservatory.

Cheekwood Botanical Garden *(Admission)*

1200 Forest Park Dr., Nashville, TN 37205 (615) 353-2148

This fifty-five acre site includes the original Cheek gardens, Japanese garden, herb garden, perennial gardens, award-winning wildflower garden, pools and water gardens, dogwood garden, fountains, meandering pathways, and a fantastic sculpture trail.

Core Arboretum *(Free)*

Monongahela Blvd., Morgantown, WV 26506 (304) 293-5201 x2547

A 91-acre arboretum on the campus of West Virginia University. Visitors enjoy 3.5 miles of walking trails in wooded areas and good birding, as well as expansive lawns planted with specimen trees.

Edisto Memorial Gardens *(Free)*

2658 U.S. Highway 301, Orangeburg, SC 29116 (803) 533-6020

First developed in the 1920s, this beautiful garden includes more than fifty beds of roses, azalea garden, wetlands park, butterfly garden, sensory garden, and a boat dock along the Edisto River.

Maymont Park *(Donation Accepted)*

2201 Shields Lake Dr., Richmond, VA 23220 (804) 358-7166

One hundred acres of high bluffs, massive rock outcroppings, streams, and ravines. Expansive lawns and specialty gardens—including Italian, Japanese, cactus, herb, butterfly, vegetable, daylily—plus unique features like shrub labyrinth and rare grotto garden make this a must-see!

Rip Van Winkle Gardens *(Admission)*

5505 Rip Van Winkle Rd., New Iberia, LA 70560 (337) 359-8525

Series of small interlocking gardens on a twenty-five acre estate. Among the overarching live oaks are collections of delicate camellias, Japanese garden, modern rose garden, and more among subtropical plantings of bamboo, banana plants, magnolias, and palms.

Lighting the Way for Papa Noel

For over a century, the Christmas Eve bonfires on the levees of south Louisiana parishes have lit up the night skies as one of the South's unique outdoor holiday traditions.

The river road between New Orleans and Baton Rouge follows the levee banks of the mighty Mississippi River, home to Cajun (Acadian) families originally expelled from Canada and forced to find a new life. Many were sent to Haiti and Jamaica, others to work the plantations as slaves. Some escaped through the wilderness and followed the river to Louisiana, a French colony, where they vowed to meet up once again. Those who finally settled along the swamps, bayous, and river parishes made a good living as hunters, trappers, and fishermen.

There are many stories about the origin of the Christmas Eve levee fires, but this is one of our favorites. Christmas was always an important time for the religious Cajuns but it held a measure of sadness, as they remembered their scattered families and prayed for their safe reunion. To dispel their sorrow, the men and boys would gather wood and pile it into big bonfire piles along the levees. On Christmas Eve they would light the fires to help their families find their way back. They knew that Papa Noel would tell their scattered loved ones to follow the lights to find their new home. As the years went by, more families found their way to Louisiana and as they were reunited with their kin, more bonfires were built along the levees.

Now, thousands of people come every Christmas to see hundred of bonfires light the dark night skies beside miles of the Mississippi on both sides of the river. Most families light their fires between 6 to 7 pm, and New Orleans-based steamboats run special excursions to view the bonfires from the water. You can be sure to hear many stories told over bowls of gumbo if you walk the river road next Christmas Eve and stop to visit and remember.

> Mistletoe is well known to most Southerners; it's the parasitic plant often used to decorate holiday homes. Its name comes from Anglo-Saxon words meaning "dung on a twig" because ancients believed mistletoe was propagated by bird droppings. It's also considered a symbol of life, fertility, and an aphrodisiac. There's a joke in there somewhere.

Low Care, No Care, Tried and True Winners

By no means a comprehensive list, these annuals are practically bullet-proof and have proven to be beautiful and low-maintenance winners in the Southern garden.

Black-eyed Susan	*Rudbeckia hirta*
Castor Bean	*Ricinus communis*
Celosia	*Celosia argentea* var. *cristata*
Cleome	*Cleome hassleriana*
Coleus	*Solenostemon scutellarioides*
Copper Plant	*Acalypha wilkesiana*
Coreopsis	*Coreopsis species*
Cosmos	*Cosmos sulphureus*
Dusty Miller	*Senecio cinerariar*
Globe Amaranth	*Gomphrena globosa*
Johnny Jump-Up	*Viola tricolor*
Joseph's Coat	*Alternanthera ficoidea*
Larkspur	*Consolida ambigua*
Melampodium	*Melampodium paludosum*
Mexican Sunflower	*Tithonia rotundifolia*
Moss Rose	*Portulaca grandiflora*
Okra (Ornamental)	*Abelmoschus esculentus*
Pansy	*Viola* x *wittrockiana*
Pentas	*Pentas lanceolata*
Pepper (Ornamental)	*Capsicum annuum*
Perilla	*Perilla frutescens*
Periwinkle	*Catharanthus roseus*
Petunia	*Petunia* x *hybrida*
Salvia	*Salvia splendens*
Sunflower	*Helianthus annuus*
Sweet Potato Vine	*Ipomoea batatas*
Zinnia	*Zinnia elegans*

Black-Eyed Susan

Zinnia

(Source: *Tough Plants for Southern Gardens* by Felder Rushing, Cool Springs Press, 2003.)

CHASING WATERFALLS

What is it about falling water that fascinates us so? After all, it's just water, right? It may be something different for each of us, but the fact remains that we seek them out, and return often, counting them as our favorite spots ... as well they should be, given a few cautions: wet rocks are slippery! And if a waterfall is fenced off, it's for your safety. Many waterfalls are in wild, remote regions, so be very careful. Here are some great ones.

1) Whitewater Falls, North Carolina

At 411 feet, Whitewater Falls, in Sumter National Forest near Cashiers, is the highest North American waterfall east of the Rocky Mountains.

2) Fall Creek Falls, Tennessee

With a sheer drop of 256 feet, this beautiful punchbowl is in Fall Creek Falls State Park near Pikeville.

3) Toccoa Falls, Georgia

On the campus of Toccoa Falls College in Toccoa, this magnificent 186-footer is easy to get to—right through the campus gift shop!

4) Noccalula Falls, Alabama

This spectacular box falls in Noccalula Falls Park near Gadsden cascades over 90 feet into a beautiful ravine.

5) Cumberland Falls, Kentucky

This falls—a 68-foot drop with a 125-foot-wide lip that earns it the nickname "Little Niagra"—is on the Cumberland River in Cumberland Falls State Park, near Corbin.

6) Hemmed In Hollow Falls, Arkansas

At 225-feet, this falls is one of the highest waterfalls between the Rockies and the Appalachians.

7) Blackwater Falls, West Virginia

Blackwater Falls State Park features this gorgeous, 66-foot falls of dark amber colored water. A paved trail makes viewing accessible to everyone.

8) Bridal Veil Falls, North Carolina

You can actually drive your car underneath this 60-foot falls on the scenic mountain highway US 64!

9) *Rainbow Falls, South Carolina*

An 80-foot falls against a granite backdrop. It's impressive but people have fallen to their deaths—be careful.

10) *Whiteoak Falls, Virginia*

A challenging trail in the Shenandoah National Park leads to a 86-foot falls; there are actually six different falls of various heights.

RUBY FALLS

Located near Chattanooga, TN, Ruby Falls is a 145 ft. waterfall 1,120 feet underground—America's largest underground waterfall.

Types of Waterfalls

- Block: water spills from a wide source.
- Cascade: water descends a series of rock steps.
- Cataract: a very high waterfall.
- Fan: water spreads out as it nears the bottom; remains in contact with bedrock.
- Horsetail: water maintains some contact with bedrock.
- Plunge: water spills over the edge, losing contact with the bedrock surface.
- Punchbowl: water is compact as it spills, then spreads out in a pool.
- Segmented: water descends in distinctly separate sections.
- Tiered: a series of waterfalls.
- Multistep: series of descending waterfalls, each with a pool.

A Cascade.

THE MOONBOW AT CUMBERLAND FALLS

An interesting thing happens at Cumberland Falls (Kentucky) on nights when the moon is full: the mist rises and a nighttime rainbow is created. One of only a handful of places in the world where this happens reliably (Victoria Falls in Zimbabwe, sometimes Yosemite Falls in California, and Middle Falls in New York are others), the lunar rainbow is best seen in fall and winter.

Cumberland Falls

SAVING THE LONGLEAF PINE

The legendary longleaf pine (*Pinus palustris*) once covered more than 90 million acres across the South. Rivaling South and Central American rainforests for biodiversity, longleaf pine ecosystems can contain over 40 plant species per square yard, and support over 30 endangered species, such as the red-cockaded woodpecker and gopher tortoise. Due to heavy logging, clearing land for development and farming, conversion to faster-growing pine species, and suppression of natural fires that once burned through the forests every two to four years, the longleaf pine forests have declined by over 97%. Today less than three million acres remain across the South, but people are working to restore the longleaf.

The longleaf pine is a particularly hardy species, able to withstand strong winds and ice storms, and is resistant to most insects and diseases that attack other pines. Taking up to 150 years to reach its full size, it often lives 300 years or more. The longleaf pine is not only more tolerant of fire than loblolly or slash pine, it actually *requires* fire for its survival. Clearing forest litter by fire every few years reduces competitive species and allows longleaf pine seeds to germinate. In turn, the cleared forest becomes home for wild turkeys, fox squirrels, quail, the red-cockaded woodpecker, and lots of other wildlife.

The longleaf pine is the official state tree of North Carolina and Alabama.

The U.S. Fish and Wildlife Service is working with conservation groups and landowners to restore longleaf pine habitat on over 57,000 acres across the South. The Nature Conservancy was awarded management of the historic Greenwood Plantation in Thomas County, Georgia, in 2002. This 5,200 acre plantation features a 1,000 acre section of unspoiled old-growth longleaf pine, where trees range in age up to 500 years old. Slowly, the habitat of the longleaf pine is being restored as people recognize this stately tree's intrinsic value.

"Culture springs from the actions of people in a landscape, and what we, especially Southerners, are watching is a daily erosion of unique folkways as our native ecosystems and all their inhabitants disappear." From *Ecology of a Cracker Childhood* by Janisse Ray; an evocative memoir to the South that is a mix of family, nature, and culture.

In the nineteenth century, longleaf pine forests were the source of naval stores—tar, pitch, turpentine and rosin—by-products used extensively in early ship-building. The slow-growing trees produced tall timber of great strength that was shipped all over the world.

Pigs with an
ATTITUDE
PROBLEM

Arkansas has been known for its razorback hogs since the days of early European settlers, who arrived with domestic swine to provide fresh pork "on the hoof." Because there was no refrigeration, settlers let the pigs forage in the forests until they needed to butcher them.

Many pigs escaped and began interbreeding with their wild counterparts. They became known as razorbacks because of their long, bristly hair, high shoulders, sloping rump, long, rangy legs and small hips. Their massive, wedge-shaped head and pointed snout made them ruthless rooting machines, voraciously digging up whole fields of crops.

Their reputation grew as the meanest hogs in the world. It's been said that the only thing worse than a razorback with an attitude, is a razorback sow at any time of the day or night! They are especially aggressive when cornered; wary, intelligent, and constantly on the move, even when feeding. They can travel at 35 mph, and pose a hot challenge for hunters. Always shoot to kill! An injured razorback is a crazed demon.

These wild hogs exist in over fifty Arkansas counties and pose many environmental problems. They eat many small mammals, destroy ground-nesting bird habitat, uproot plants, and destroy waterholes and vegetation. According to the Arkansas Game and Fish Commission, hogs may be taken during open hunting seasons as long as they are roaming freely on public lands and the weapon used is legal for the season. Feral hogs can also transmit brucellosis and trichinosis, so game hunters should always cook the meat well.

However, *some* people think a pig with an attitude problem is a *good* thing. The University of Arkansas mascot has been the Razorbacks since 1910, following an impressive victory of 16–0 over Louisiana State. Arkansas Coach

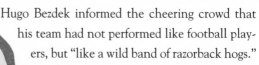

Hugo Bezdek informed the cheering crowd that his team had not performed like football players, but "like a wild band of razorback hogs." The name stuck and the college proudly voted to change their official mascot from the Cardinals to the Razorbacks. The current official live mascot is a 380 pound Russian boar named Tusk, which closely resembles a wild razorback hog. Tusk attends all Arkansas home games, as every loyal fan should. Woooooooooo, Pig! Sooie!! Go Hogs!

Arkansas is an outdoor wonder. The state has more than 600,000 acres of lakes and more than 9,700 miles of rivers and streams. There are 6 national parks, two and a half million acres of national forest, seven national scenic byways, three state scenic byways, and fifty state parks.

Johnny Cash was born in Kingsland, Arkansas.

Sam Walton founded Wal-Mart in Rogers, Arkansas, in 1962. Its sales at the close of 2005 exceeded $312 billion dollars.

The origin of the state name is thought to be derived from a French translation of the Sioux word *acansa*, meaning downstream place.

The Language of Herbs

Many people know that flowers have a secret language, popularized during the Victorian period. For example, a yellow rose is said to signify jealousy, while an iris represents hope. Entire conversations could be carried on in this hidden language by using flowers to express emotions. But what is less well known is that herbs also have a hidden language of their own. Can we talk?

Parsley

Basil

Basil	fidelity, love
Borage	courage
Calendula	peace and harmony
Chamomile	humility and patience
Chives	usefulness
Coriander	secret value
Dill	tranquility
Horehound	health
Hyssop	sacrifice
Lavender	distrust
Lemon balm	sympathy
Marjoram	happiness
Mint	hospitality, virtue, and wisdom
Parsley	festivity
Pennyroyal	go away
Rosemary	remembrance
Sage	high esteem, long life
Tansy	hostility
Thyme	strength and courage
Yarrow	healing of the heart

Rosemary

Thyme

(Source: *The Southern Garden Advisor*, by Barabara Pleasant, Cool Springs Press, 2003)

MAMMOTH CAVING

Spe*what*?? Spelunking—pronounced pretty much the way it's spelled—is the hobby of exploring caves, while caving is the term reserved for more serious cave explorers. The South is full of caves, especially Tennessee, Alabama, Kentucky, and Georgia. Water erodes the soft limestone between granite shelves to create underground labyrinths, sometimes large ones. Serious cavers thrive on the challenge of crawling through narrow spaces, inching along rock ledges, rappelling into darkened pits, clambering up walls, and splashing through underground streams.

Caves open to the general public, like Mammoth Cave in Kentucky, allow comfortable exploration by people of all ages and abilities. Mammoth Cave offers over a dozen different caving tours, from 30 minute to 6 hour treks.

Mammoth Cave National Park, Kentucky www.nps.gov/maca/home.htm

If you're caving, don't forget your:

- Hardhat
- 3 sources of light, (preferably 2 headlamps, a small flashlight, and extra batteries)
- Old hiking boots
- Knee or elbow pads
- Bottled water
- Old clothes–long pants and long sleeves
- Bandanas–good for keeping cave crickets out of your hair
- Rope
- Companions—it's standard cave safety to go with at least one or two other people. Cave passages can be confusing; pay attention to navigational features to avoid becoming lost. Leave word behind so others know when you left, where you're going, and when you expect to return.

THE PONIES OF CHINCOTEAGUE

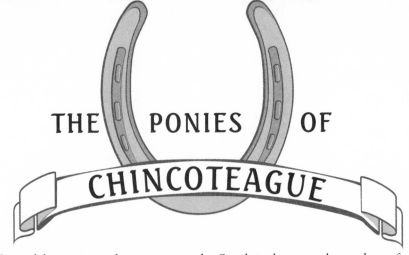

One of the great outdoor events in the South is the annual round-up of the wild ponies of Chincoteague. Every horse-loving child of the South has read *Misty of Chincoteague* by Marguerite Henry and can practically recite the entire text. But if you're not familiar with the tale, by all means, read on.

Most of the year, herds of wild horses graze the windswept dunes and marsh grasses and wander the beaches and trails on Assateague Island, off the Virginia coast. According to legend, the horses swam ashore from a Spanish galleon, which shipwrecked on the treacherous shoals and sank.

A more likely origin is that these small but sturdy horses are descendants of early settlers' herds, set loose on the island in the 1600s to graze naturally (and thereby avoid fencing taxes). The mainly pinto ponies are a strong and hardy breed, averaging 14 to 15 hands high. By the 1700s, pony penning (the round-up) had become an annual event, complete with festivities and fun for the whole community. Livestock owners gathered to round-up and brand their loose herds on both Assateague and also its neighboring Chincoteague Island. The penning and subsequent auctions were held first on one island, then on the next.

The "swimming of the ponies" began in the early 1920s when a wealthy landowner bought the southern end of Assateague Island. Because this cut off most villagers' access to the oyster beds, most people moved to the smaller and more protected Chincoteague Island. The pony penning also moved to Chincoteague, and a new tradition of driving the wild ponies across the channel from Assateague to Chincoteague began.

The annual festival began as a way to raise money for the volunteer fire department. It soon started attracting thousands of visitors, who come to watch the herds swim the channel for the annual penning. Today the pony penning is held every July during the Chincoteague Volunteer Firemen's Carnival, when "saltwater cowboys" drive the herds across Assateague Channel at low tide. The pony auction raises money for the fire company but it also helps thin the herd, which is limited to 150 on Assateague Island (now a wildlife refuge). Horse races, wild horse rides, carnival attractions, nightly entertainment, and the pony auction are part of the festivities. The day after the auction, spectators gather to watch the herd swim back to Assateague.

The Death of Blackbeard

During his reign upon the seas, the infamous pirate Blackbeard plundered the coasts off Virginia and the Carolinas. According to legend, it was at Ocracoke Inlet that Blackbeard's luck ran out. North Carolinians had grown tired of Blackbeard's campaigns against them and appealed to Virginia Governor Spotswood for help (possibly because Blackbeard had shared his booty with North Carolina Governor Eden). On November 22, 1718, the English navy attacked. In the battle, Blackbeard suffered more than thirty major wounds (mostly from being hacked by sword cuts). After his death, Blackbeard's head was cut off and hung up for all to see.

Diamonds Are Forever

A rare opportunity exists for rockhounds and treasure hunters. The Crater of Diamonds State Park in Arkansas is the *only* diamond-producing site *in the world* open to the public.

Not only can you dig for diamonds, but park rangers will help identify your finds, provide you with a list of reputable diamond cutters, and allow you to keep your diamond!

The first diamonds were found in the area in August 1906 by John Huddleston. He had bought his 160-acre farm just several months earlier, and his find started a diamond rush as soon as word got out. A big find in similar peridotite soil in the South African Kimberleys in 1889 prompted locals to suspect there might be diamonds in Arkansas, but none had been found until Huddleston's accidental sighting.

He sold the diamond-bearing land for $36,000 and several mining companies tried their luck for a number of years with mixed results. In 1972 the State of Arkansas paid $750,000 and bought the land for a state park, and it's been a free-for-all ever since.

Scientists believe most of Arkansas was under water 300 billion years ago, except for the Ouachita Mountains. About 100 million years ago the continents finished their major continental drift, but the last movements caused cracks in the earth's crust, allowing hot magma to escape. This volcanic activity pushed diamonds up from deep within the earth, where they'd been formed under tremendous heat and pressure.

Diamonds found at the crater are typically smooth and well rounded. They are translucent, most commonly white, yellow, or brown, and average the size of a match head. Three methods of searching are practiced at Crater of Diamonds—scouring the surface, especially after a hard rain; digging down 6 to 12 inches and sifting the soil through a screen; or digging deep holes and hand sorting concentrated gravel in screens.

Finds are impressive enough to encourage anyone to go diamond hunting. Recorded finds in 2005 totaled 536, and over the years several famous diamonds have come from the Arkansas crater. On permanent display at the Crater of Diamonds State Park is the most perfect diamond the American Gem Society has ever certified. Found in 1990, the "Strawn-Wagner" diamond weighed 3.03 carats in the rough and 1.09 when cut. The "Amarillo Starlight" diamond, an impressive 16.37 carats, is the largest diamond ever unearthed by a park visitor since the crater became a state park in 1972.

The Strawn-Wagner Diamond is the most perfect diamond the AGS has ever certified.

Crater of Diamonds State Park is located in Murfreesboro, Arkansas, which is about 120 miles from Little Rock. Take I-30 to Arkadelphia, then hang a turn south on ARK 26 to Murfreesboro; you can't miss it. If you don't want to get rich and famous digging diamonds (though we find this hard to comprehend), then you can camp, fish, hike, observe wildlife, or splash around at the water park on the park grounds.

The "Uncle Sam" diamond, a 40.23 carat white diamond discovered at the Crater of Diamonds State Park in 1924, is the largest diamond ever found in North America.

Diamonds are weighed in points. Points are 1/100 of a caret; thus, a .50 caret diamond weighs 50 points.

So Close, Yet So Far

Even though diamonds and coal are composed of carbon, that's about their only similarity. Coal results from compacted vegetation while diamonds were formed under conditions of extremely high pressure and heat, deep within the earth.

What's in a Name?

You don't have to be a Latin scholar to be a great gardener, but understanding the basics of the plant naming system is informative and it can really be fun! Every plant has a name—usually Latin—that identifies it and only it. The first part is the genus (think of it as the "generic" or family name). The second name is the species (or the "specific"name), which will identify the type of individual plant. Both are italic, initial upper case for the genus, and initial lower case for the species. (A possible third name may be a cultivar; it's enclosed within single quotes like this, *Acer rubrum* 'October Glory' and refers to a superior selection.) The really cool thing is that you'll quickly pick up clues as to what the plant is like. For example:

alba	= white
japonica	= originating in Japan
canadensis	= originating in Canada
citrinus	= lemon yellow color
lancifolia	= lance-shaped
crispula	= curled
undulata	= wavy
micro	= very small
serrata	= serrated leaves
variegata	= variegated
sempervirens	= evergreen
gracilis	= graceful

(Source: adapted from *Tennessee Gardener's Guide*, *Third Edition*, Judy Lowe, Cool Springs Press, 2001)